COUNTRY MUSIC

Other Recent Works by Charles Wright

Halflife: Improvisations & Interviews,
1977–87

The World of the Ten Thousand Things:
Poems, 1980–1990

Chickamauga

Quarter Notes:
Improvisations and Interviews

COUNTRY MUSIC

SELECTED EARLY POEMS

CHARLES WRIGHT

SECOND EDITION
With a Foreword by David St. John

WESLEYAN UNIVERSITY PRESS

Published by University Press of New England
Hanover and London

Wesleyan University Press
Published by University Press of New England, Hanover, NH 03755

Acknowledgment is gratefully made to the following periodicals, in the pages of which all the poems in this book were first published: *The American Poetry Review*: "Autumn," "Saturday 6 a.m.," "Tattoos"; *The American Review*: "Dog," "1975," "Snapshot"; *Antaeus*: "Going Home," "'Where Moth and Rust Doth Corrupt'"; *Arena*: "Nocturne," "Storm"; *The Atlantic Monthly*: "April"; *The Barataria Review*: "Easter, 1974"; *The Chicago Review*: "Death," "Indian Summer," "January," "Quotidiana"; *Choice*: "Him," "The Poet Grows Older"; *Cold Spring Journal*: "Reply to Chi K'ang"; *Crazy Horse*: "Grace"; *Field*: "Born Again," "Captain Dog," "Dino Campana," "Invisible Landscape," "Morandi," "Self-Portrait in 2035," "Snow"; *Greenhouse Review*: "Moving On"; *Grove*: "Spider Crystal Ascension," "Thinking of Georg Trakl"; *Hearse*: "Yellow"; *The Iowa Review*: "Anniversary," "Homage to Arthur Rimbaud," "Homage to X," "Reply to Lapo Gianni," "12 Lines at Midnight"; *Lillabulero*: "Delta Traveller," "White"; *Marilyn*: "California Twilight," "Reunion," "Depression Before the Solstice"; *The New Yorker*: "Childhood," "Clear Night," "Edvard Munch," "Homage to Baron Corvo," "Homage to Ezra Pound," "Noon," "Remembering San Zeno," "Rural Route," "Sentences," "Stone Canyon Nocturne"; *The Oberlin Quarterly*: "The Voyage"; *The Ohio Review*: "At Zero," "Bays Mountain Covenant," "Cancer Rising," "Virgo Descending," "Wishes"; *Occident*: "Next"; *The Partisan Review*: "Link Chain"; *Ploughshares*: "Sex"; *Pocket Pal*: "Bygones"; *Poetry*: "Blackwater Mountain," "Chinoiserie," "Clinchfield Station," "Congenital," "Dog Creek Mainline," "Negatives," "Nightdream," "Northhanger Ridge," "Skins," "The Fever Toy"; *Poetry Northwest*: "Aubade"; *The Pomegranate Press Broadsides*: "Equation," "Nerval's Mirror"; *Red Weather*: "Signature"; *The Seneca Review*: "Slides of Verona"; *Skywriting*: "Primogeniture," "Sky Valley Rider"; *The Southern Poetry Review*: "Hardin County"; *The Southern Review*: "Homage to Baron Corvo" and "Homage to Ezra Pound"; *Three Rivers Poetry Journal*: "Cloud River."

The poems "Aubade," "The Poet Grows Older," "The Voyage," "Nocturne," and "Storm" were published in Canada in 1968 by The House of Anansi Press of Toronto in a limited edition of a booklet entitled *The Dream Ammal* and are copyrighted in Canada by the publisher.

The poems "Definitions," "Firstborn," "The New Poem," "Nocturne," "Notes for Oscar Wilde at San Miniato," "One Two Three," and "Oscar Wilde at San Miniato" first appeared in *The Venice Notebook*, published by the Barn Dream Press of Boston in 1971.

Cover and frontispiece illustration: *1960, Landscape*, pencil drawing on paper, Raccolta Tavoni, Bologna, by Morandi. Reproduced from *Morandi, Drawings*, by N. Pozza, by permission of Franca May Edizioni.

Printed in the United States of America   5   4   3

CIP data appear at the end of the book

For Holly, SMB

"The country was always better
than the people."

—Ernest Hemingway

CONTENTS

Foreword: "Charles Wright's *Country Music*"
   by David St. John / xiii
Preface / xxiii

The Grave of the Right Hand

Aubade / 3
The Poet Grows Older / 4
The Voyage / 5
Nocturne / 6
Storm / 7

Hard Freight

Homage to Ezra Pound / 11
Homage to Arthur Rimbaud / 13
Homage to Baron Corvo / 14
Homage to X / 16
The New Poem / 17
Portrait of the Poet in
   Abraham von Werdt's Dream / 18
Chinoiserie / 19
One Two Three / 20
White / 21
Firstborn / 22
Slides of Verona / 28
Grace / 29
Negatives / 30
The Fever Toy / 31

Notes for Oscar Wilde
    at San Miniato / 32

Oscar Wilde at San Miniato / 33

Nocturne / 34

Yellow / 35

Dog Creek Mainline / 36

Blackwater Mountain / 38

Sky Valley Rider / 39

Sex / 41

Northhanger Ridge / 42

Primogeniture / 44

Nightdream / 45

Congenital / 47

Clinchfield Station / 48

Bloodlines

Virgo Descending / 51

Easter, 1974 / 53

Cancer Rising / 54

Tattoos / 56

Notes to Tattoos / 76

Hardin County / 77

Delta Traveller / 79

Skins / 82

Notes to Skins / 102

Link Chain / 103

Bays Mountain Covenant / 106

Rural Route / 107

China Trace

Childhood / 111

Snow / 112

Self-Portrait in 2035 / 113

Morandi / 114

Dog / 115

Snapshot / 116

Indian Summer / 117

Wishes / 118

Quotidiana / 119

At Zero / 120

Sentences / 121

Death / 122

Next / 123

January / 124

1975 / 125

Nerval's Mirror / 126

Edvard Munch / 127

Bygones / 128

Equation / 129

California Twilight / 130

Anniversary / 131

12 Lines at Midnight / 132

Dino Campana / 133

Invisible Landscape / 134

Remembering San Zeno / 135

Born Again / 136

Captain Dog / 137

Depression Before
    the Solstice / 138

Stone Canyon Nocturne / 139

Reply to Chi K'ang / 140

Reunion / 141

"Where Moth and Rust
    Doth Corrupt" / 142

April / 143

Signature / 144

Noon / 145

Going Home / 146

Cloud River / 147

Reply to Lapo Gianni / 148

Thinking of Georg Trakl / 149

Spider Crystal Ascension / 150

Moving On / 151

Clear Night / 152

Autumn / 153

Sitting at Night
    on the Front Porch / 154

Saturday 6 a.m. / 155

Him / 156

Charles Wright's COUNTRY MUSIC

It has been ten years since the first edition of Charles Wright's *Country Music: Selected Early Poems,* which gathers work from his first four collections of poetry: *The Grave of the Right Hand, Hard Freight, Bloodlines,* and *China Trace.* In that time, Wright has dazzled his readers with four more quite extraordinary new volumes: *The Southern Cross, The Other Side of the River, Zone Journals,* and *Xionia,* which have now been collected into one volume entitled *The World of the Ten Thousand Things.* For the many readers who have been longtime admirers of his poetry, it has been gratifying to note that the critical reception to Charles Wright's work has also kept pace with the widening of his audience, an audience which has been increasingly drawn to his poetry by its great power and beauty, its incisive spirituality and meditative elegance.

Certainly, the fact that Helen Vendler, David Kalstone, Peter Stitt, Calvin Bedient and others have championed his poetry in their thoughtful and perceptive reviews has helped this audience at large to recognize that Charles Wright is without question one of our preeminent American poets. His many prizes, including the 1983 National Book Award for *Country Music,* The Academy of American Poets' Edgar Allan Poe Award, and the Brandeis Creative Arts Citation for Poetry, have also shown the high regard in which he's held by his peers. Yet it strikes me that Charles Wright's poetry is highly unusual in that it stands not only in the context of its own time (and such temporal accolades), but that its lucid illuminations are also intended to reflect far into—while casting light upon—those dark recesses of our futures. For his readers, Charles Wright's poetry often serves as a kind of prayer book, a kind of poetic hymnal or speculative field guide we might carry with us on our own metaphysical journeys.

Over the past twenty years Charles Wright has written an impressive and demanding body of work that can stand in its accomplishments as the equal of *any* poet's in the latter part of the twentieth century. This has been not only an artistic achievement of notable dimension but a spiritual one as well. Quite simply, Charles Wright has emerged as the most visionary American poet since Hart Crane; he is that most rare of poets—one who is stylistically (and tirelessly) inventive, yet who speaks to and from a tradition that harkens back to Dante. With the mirror of his collection *The World of the Ten Thousand Things* so recently before us, it seems to me a proper occasion to look back at the rich and complex harmonies of Charles Wright's selected early poetry, *Country Music*.

* * *

Throughout his career, Charles Wright has been a highly adept literary architect; he is not only a formal master, he is also an endlessly imaginative sculptor of larger unifying structures for his work. *China Trace*, Wright's fourth full collection, completed the triptych of books begun with *Hard Freight* (his second volume) and which he'd continued through his much praised third book, *Bloodlines*. In *Country Music*, Wright has selected only five brief prose poems from his first book, *The Grave of the Right Hand*, as a kind of prologue to this triptych of his subsequent books.

It has always seemed natural to me (after the finely crafted, visually acute and precise poems of his debut volume) that Wright should feel the need to gather his past, in some sense to write—and rewrite—not only that past, but also the self (the poetic self and voice) which he was bringing to maturity in his newer and more ambitious poems. Clearly, in terms of both style and subject matter, this new direction was signaled by the poem "Dog Creek Mainline" from the book *Hard Freight*. Knotty, rhythmically muscular, alliterative, yet still highly imagistic and visual, Wright's poetry took on a beautiful rasping quality; his work began more deliberately to reflect the abstract concerns embodied in his retrieval of the past, all the while exhibiting the enjambed music that seemed to arise so magically from his lines. Wright also began revealing in these new poems from *Hard Freight* and *Bloodlines* his self-conscious choice to use both overt and covert autobiographical subject matter. These now familiar impulses in Wright's poetry began to grow, it seems, along with his conviction that the "unknown," or the spiritual and metaphysical, could best be encountered or mediated through the "known." For Wright this meant a reclamation of his past, an attempt at the recuperation of his childhood, was necessary before he could begin to look toward the yearnings and desirings of the "*beyond*" we find so delicately considered in the volume *China Trace*, the final panel of Wright's triptych.

In *Hard Freight* (and to some extent in the poems of *Bloodlines*) familial memories and episodes of Wright's youth in Tennessee and North Carolina mix quite easily—"naturally" we might say—with the rich landscapes of their settings. Yet, in *Bloodlines*, Wright begins the rigorous process of not only attempting to orient himself to his past, now as a mature speaker, but of orienting himself in relation to his own *present* and *presence* as well. *Bloodlines* is a fiercely elegiac book, detailing the losses of people, places, and times that have passed out of the poet's life. In addition to the powerful elegies for his parents, Wright provides a double axis of personal reckoning to *Bloodlines*; the intimate losses of the book revolve around two masterful poetic sequences, "Tattoos" and "Skins" (each consists of twenty numbered sections and each sequence serves to echo the concerns of the other).

"Tattoos" illustrates a list of psychologically potent events which have, each in some distinct way, "marked" Wright. "Skins" is a highly abstract inquiry into the materials of existence, from the most elemental to the most ethereal. The philosophical and metaphysical issues of "Skins" combine in a complex verbal music. And even though he questions his own ordering of the present, Wright nevertheless attempts to lay to rest his reclamation of the past while looking toward the certain—if ill-defined—terrain of his future, a terrain which takes as its horizon Wright's own death. Although, in *China Trace*, Wright will ask what may exist beyond that horizon (albeit in his own yearnings and imaginings), it is in *Bloodlines*, at the end of the final section of "Skins," that the meditations found in *China Trace* really begin:

> And what does it come to, Pilgrim,
> This walking to and fro on the earth, knowing
> That nothing changes, or everything;
> And only, to tell it, these sad marks,
> Phrases half-parsed, ellipses and scratches across the dirt?
> It comes to a point. It comes and it goes.

So, it is with these "sad marks" that Wright begins his attempt to tell not only what it comes to, but where—and why—his pilgrimage must continue.

* * *

China Trace remains one of the most remarkable books of American poetry of recent years. Though made up of individual pieces, *China Trace* functions also as a single book-length poem, beginning with the speaker's childhood and concluding with his assumption into the sky, into what Wright has called "a man-made heaven." *China Trace* is a personal history pushed toward its future; its speaker reaches toward his own death and the desired salvation it may or may not bring. In the course of these poems, Wright often clearly does *not* believe, yet he feels called upon to continue the search that his spiritual yearnings have prompted. The book is filled with portents of what's to come, as in the poems "Next" ("I want to lie down, I am so tired, and let / The crab grass seep through my heart, / Side by side with the inchworm and the fallen psalm . . .") and "January" ("In some other life / I'll stand where I'm standing now, and will look down, and will see / My own face, and not know what I'm looking at"). Much as in the poem "Skins," it is the elemental regeneration of a life—its death into decay, the body passing through its cycle of water, earth, fire, and air—which seems as much as one might ask of salvation. Here in "Self-Portrait in 2035" is Charles Wright imagining himself at 100 years old:

> The root becomes him, the road ruts
> That are sift and grain in the powderlight
> Recast him, sink bone in him,
> Blanket and creep up, fine, fine:
>
> Worm-waste and pillow tick; hair
> Prickly and dust-dangled, his arms and black shoes
> Unlinked and laceless, his face false
> In the wood-rot, and past pause . . .
>
> Darkness, erase these lines, forget these words.
> Spider recite his one sin.

The poems in *China Trace* are often offered as small cosmologies, many posited by Wright as approximations of both what is and what's to come. Even if, as he says in the poem "Morandi" (for the great Italian painter), it is "the void/These objects sentry for, and rise from," it is clear that the poems of *China Trace* are firmly rooted in the objects of everyday life, in the earth itself (as well as in natural landscape), and in the domestic experience reflected in the journal-like quality of many of the poems. It is no accident these poems are often fixed not only by place names, but by specific times of day or night, phases of the moon, dates, and personal references as well. In his diary of passage, the quotidian and the natural must balance what otherwise could simply seem the illusions all dreamers must perform. Thus, it remains vital to Wright that he must continuously mark and notate his search with the facts of his existence. Otherwise, without these resolutely concrete notes in the log, what future resonance could such a spiritual search have?

China Trace is a pilgrim's book, the same "Pilgrim" who is addressed at the conclusion of "Skins." It carries a strong and dramatic narrative—the soul's search for salvation, a man's yearning for the *other*. *China Trace* also shows Charles Wright to be one of the most formally inventive poets writing. The weblike structures of his poems reverberate with his characteristic verbal music, and their individual images seem to radiate through *Country Music* as a whole. *China Trace* grows slowly into a guidebook of spiritual passage, with nods to fellow travelers along the way. Sometimes, we feel that the speaker of these poems has suffered his own silence, in seclusion, for a long while. Sometimes, we listen as the poems take on the tone of a wanderer who has walked off from the tribe, the city, in order to turn and speak for it, at last. In "Depression Before the Solstice," Wright sees:

> The watchers and holy ones set out, divining
> The seal, eclipses
> Taped to their sleeves with black felt,
> Their footprints filling with sparks
> In the bitter loam behind them, ahead of them stobbed
>   with sand,
> And walk hard, and regret nothing.

Many have remarked upon the hermetic tone of *China Trace*, attributing it in part to the influence of Eugenio Montale, the superb Italian poet whom Wright has translated so well. Yet the impulse to touch mystery has always been present in Wright's work. In the illuminating *instants* of *China Trace* we are in the presence— as in all of the finest religious works—of the mystery of the *one*, the individual, confronted by the expanse of the greater and more fluent *other*. Here is the poem "Stone Canyon Nocturne":

> Ancient of Days, old friend, no one believes you'll come back.
> No one believes in his own life anymore.
>
> The moon, like a dead heart, cold and unstartable, hangs by a thread
> At the earth's edge,
> Unfaithful at last, splotching the ferns and the pink shrubs.
>
> In the other world, children undo the knots in their tally strings.
> They sing songs, and their fingers blear.
>
> And here, where the swan hums in his socket, where bloodroot
> And belladonna insist on our comforting,
> Where the fox in the canyon wall empties our hands, ecstatic for more,
>
> Like a bead of clear oil the Healer revolves through the night wind,
> Part eye, part tear, unwilling to recognize us.

Once again, Wright tries to explore the nature of our proper relationship to what "lies beyond," since fear and acquiescence are both regarded as inadequate. For Wright, this simple search always leads back to language; for that reason his poetry has, over the years, developed a more heightened and extremely graphic sense of what characterizes verbal enactment. As a result, Wright has often been called "painterly" in his use of wordplay and in his execution of dazzling verbal chromatics. It is as if many of Wright's poems keep seeking some ideogrammatic form, and as such exist almost as some other language—something between the language we know and the glyphs of an obscure, yet resilient poetic cult. There is, in Charles Wright's poetry, much of the tone of Yeats' occult clarity and Rilke's sonorous passion. It's no accident that the natural elements often appear in the act of "writing" themselves across the face of the earth or the sky. It is this singularly physical signature of passage, both man's and the world's, which so intrigues Wright, perhaps because so much of his poetry reflects his struggle against the impossibility of inscription.

Certainly one can trace Pound behind some of Wright's ambitions, just as one can find echoes of Hart Crane's revisionist-symbolist impulses, or the devotional grandeur of Gerard Manley Hopkins. Yet I'm convinced that, in the forging of this new line and new language for himself, Charles Wright has responded to a tremendously personal, *internal* pressure—a pressure to discover the proper word construct, the right syllable mobile, the most pleasing sound ladder—in his search for an appropriate aesthetic to reflect and convey his anxious, metaphysical explorations.

There is some risk, certainly, when so demanding a notion of language is coupled with so abstract a subject matter. But Charles Wright is an impeccable stylist, and his poems remain rooted in real experience even while seeking some greater, perhaps more universal, equation.

Country Music as a whole "traces" Charles Wright's grand passions: his desire to reclaim and redeem a personal past, to make a reckoning with his present, and to conjure the terms by which we might face the future. If we wonder where the road of these poems can possibly end, it is the end we knew would be reached from the very beginning. If we wonder what will become of the "Pilgrim" who has disguised himself so often as "I," "You," and "He," then we are answered in the final poem of *China Trace*, with its devotional pun on hymn, "Him":

His sorrow hangs like a heart in the star-flowered boundary tree.
It mirrors the endless wind.

He feeds on the lunar differences and flies up at the dawn.

When he lies down, the waters will lie down with him,
And all that walks and all that stands still, and sleep through the thunder.

It's for him that the willow bleeds.

Look for him high in the flat black of the northern Pacific sky,
Released in his suit of lights,
                lifted and laid clear.

*   *   *

In *Country Music* we see the same explosive imagery, the same dismantled and concentric (or parallel) narratives, the same resolutely spiritual concerns that have become so familiar to us in Wright's more recent poetry. The idea of using a fluid "journal" construct, which becomes the central formal aspect of *The World of the Ten Thousand Things*, can be discovered in the poems of *China Trace*. The charged verbal rhythms and the crystalline music that have become hallmarks of Wright's poetry both have their poetic workbooks contained in *Country Music*. And it is here, especially in those poems of overt autobiographical reckoning, that we come to recognize the importance of Charles Wright as an American poet, most specifically as a Southern poet. The "country" in *Country Music* is meant to signal a fierce regionalism in Wright, as well as to honor the "lyric, the human theme" of country music itself, an art whose story line, Wright says, seldom varies: "change your life or else heaven won't be your home." Yet the title also announces the importance of understanding how elements of landscape in Charles Wright's poems have been first remembered and recovered, then precisely reinvented and constructed as poetic entities (and melodies). In his prose book, *Halflife*, Wright says of his poems from *Zone Journals* something that is applicable to all of his work, that his poems "are about language and landscape, and how they coexist in each other, and speak for, and to, each other." In his poetry, Wright looks to the landscapes that have nourished him, contained him, and inspired him, and tries to give them worthy poetic voices.

We need also to keep in mind the interwoven quality of Wright's spiritual aspirations with the poetic materials of his poems. In Charles Wright's poetry, reticence is a kind of faith and style is an articulation of virtue. As Wright says elsewhere in *Halflife*, "True vision is great style." Wright's poems are not only truly devotional, they are each secular prayers begging to break into a realm far beyond their own seclusion or privacy.

It is perhaps Charles Wright's greatest accomplishment that, while his poems remain very much of the world, they are nevertheless resolutely spiritual in character. It is this, even more than his technical virtuosity, formal prowess, and astounding imaginative range which makes him unique among his contemporaries. Charles Wright's poetic maps are drawn with humor and tenderness, great clarity and imagistic precision; yet it is his reverberating metaphors and complex verbal overlays that continue to dazzle his readers. Like his master, Cézanne, Wright insists that the very nature of perception itself change within us, that we might see more clearly the world which is without. This remarkable volume, *Country Music,* is an essential key to understanding the delicate poetic cosmology that resonates in Charles Wright's poetry. Lastly, let me remind the reader that one of the many rewards of these poems is that they seem so often to arise, in their consummate grace and power, in voices we slowly come to recognize as the simple echoes and lost harmonies of our own.

David St. John

PREFACE

It's been ten years now since I put this collection together from my first four books. I am still, surprisingly enough, satisfied with the editorial decisions I made back then, especially as concerns my first book, *The Grave of the Right Hand*, from which I kept only a kind of prologue—five prose poems—to the "trilogy" which followed it.

A couple of structures were at work in the book's assembly. One was invisible: after the prologue, the three following sections (*Hard Freight*, *Bloodlines*, and *China Trace*) were to represent the present, past, and future, which, in fact, they more or less do. The other was more, I hope, apparent. The three parts were organized within themselves as, first, a disparate collection of poems; second, a group of poems clustered around two longish "sequences"; and, third, a section, *China Trace*, to be a single long poem, an odd one, but essentially one poem composed of many chapters (forty-six in all) whose protagonist goes from one point (Childhood) to another (The Heaven of the Fixed Stars), though not always in a linear fashion.

A third framework, and surely an invisible structure at the time, was the fact that *Country Music* was one part, the first, of a two-part invention. The second part, *The World of the Ten Thousand Things*, has now appeared. Its longer, looser assemblages would not have been possible without the foreground of the compact and more condensed poems at work here: the short and the long of it that play—to my mind and intention, at least—one song.

It has been suggested that all forms possess their virtue in themselves and not in any conjectural content. I don't entirely agree with this, but I do believe such a statement contains more truth than falsehood. It has also been suggested—again by Jorge Luis Borges—that everything a man writes, in the end, traces the outlines of his own face. I find it has been that way with me.

C.W.

THE GRAVE OF THE
RIGHT HAND

Aubade

Over Govino Bay, looking up from the water's edge, the landscape resembles nothing so much as the hills above Genova, valleying into the sea, washing down olive, cypress and excessive arbutus into the slow snapping of the plane trees where I, surrendering to the pulse beat of a silence so faint that it seems to come from another country, watch the sun rise over Albania, waiting—calmly, unquestioning— for Saint Spiridion of Holy Memory to arise, leave his silver casket and emerge, wearing the embroidered slippers, from his grove of miracles above the hill.

Corfu

The Poet Grows Older

It seemed, at the time, so indifferent an age that I recall nothing of it except an infinite tedium to be endured. I envied no one, nor dreamed of anything in particular as, unwillingly, I enveloped myself in all of the various disguises of a decent childhood. Nothing now comes to mind of ever embarking upon famous voyages to the usual continents; of making, from the dark rooms and empty houses of my imagination, brilliant escapes from unnatural enemies; or, on rainy winter afternoons in an attic, of inventing one plot or counterplot against a prince or a beast. . . . Instead, it must have been otherwise.

I try to remember, nevertheless, something of all that time and place, sitting alone here in a room in the middle of spring, hearing the sound of a rain which has fallen for most of April, concerned with such different things, things done by others. . . . I read of the aimless coups in the old dynasties from Africa to Afghanistan, their new republics whose lists of war lords alone are enough to distress the Aryan tongue; of intricate rockets in search of a planet, soon, perhaps to land in a country somewhere outside the pedestrian reach of reason; of the latest, old sailor's account of a water dragon seen bathing off the grizzled coast of Scotland. . . . It is at times such as this, and without thinking, really, clothed in my goat's-wool robes, that I steal a camel from an outlying Arabian stable, gather together my clansmen, and gallop for days along the miraculous caravan trails to Asia.

The Voyage

At first I was overly cautious, procedure being all-important. I gathered around me those I considered friends, discovering, with a certain shock, a mere handful—nothing else, however, was lacking, as I had for months assembled equipage, and such rudiments as maps of cities, tidal charts, coastal readings, cryptic dictionaries, and guides to unusual monuments. Only, in assuring readiness, I had planned too well. . . . As it was, this much should have been warning.

For days on end we waited, close by the north-east docks, admiring the stubborn tugs at work, studying the sea lanes. Such depths of perfect skies over the gaudy ships, outward-bound through the gay whistles of sea birds! . . . And at night the glide and swish of well-oiled engines, the long calls of the horns. . . . The weeks lengthened, our patience thickening. Then something altered, if imperceptibly at first: perhaps some quirk of the weather, perhaps of the sea. A little later and it was unmistakable: things tended to incline together, fogging distinctions, ships became less common, and schedules grew erratic; destinations became unsure in my head; the nights were longer, and with them there was the uncontrollable desire for sleep, up till then only vaguely recalled. Eventually, even, some of my friends, sharers of the voyage, vanished. . . .

It is so difficult to come back, perspectives blunted, and to have only the waiting, now in the shuttered light, in the clutter of objects here in this drafty attic, until all is in readiness once more. Soon, perhaps, we shall go back down. But then, what stingy cargo to reload, what slackened baggage, O my stunted puppets!

Nocturne

The weeds have thickened among the orchards and leaves dangle unnoticed under the archways. At nighttime, before, where torchlight once peeled the darkness back from the lawn mosaics, from the formal gardens, where, it has been rumored, the parties attained such a perfection that Bacchus himself, angered at certain contests staged in his name, peered in one twilight, then ordered his image stricken from the household, his paeans discontinued, all is unshingled by the moon. Occasional chords from a ghostly lute, it is true, will sometimes come down the same Alpine wind that continues to herd the small waters into the shore; or a strayed traveller, or some misguided pilgrim might, of a summer evening, if he stands quite still and says nothing, imagine he hears the slight off-rhythm of some hexameter line deep in the olive grove, as the slither of night birds moves toward the darker trees. But that is all.

Grotte di Catullo, Sirmione

Storm

And when, that night, the unseasonable rain (the hail a shredding sound in the lemon trees) thudded against the lumbering of the bay, in August, haunting the dark with a querulous whiteness, he retired to the basement room under the house to study the various aspects of water, the ships in sudden counterpoint on the rising scales of the sea, and to wait for the breakthrough, across the barren hills of his brain, of the bronze soldiers, for the swelling flash of their knives.

Positano

HARD FREIGHT

Homage to Ezra Pound

Past San Sebastiano, past
The Ogni Santi and San Trovaso, down
The Zattere and left
Across the tiered bridge to where
—Off to the right, half-hidden—
The Old Dogana burns in the spring sun:
This is how you arrive.

This is the street where Pound lives,
A cul-de-sac
Of rheumy corners and cracked stone,
At whose approach the waters
Assemble, the gulls cry out;
In here—unspeaking, unturned—he waits,
Sifting the cold affections of the blood.

                    *

Others have led the way,
Vanishing in their sleep, their beds
Unmade, the sheets still damp
From what has set them apart—
Cancer or bad lungs, the wrack
Of advancing age, the dull
Incense of suicide . . .

And he has survived,
Or refused to follow, and now
Walks in the slow strobe of the sunlight,
Or sits in his muffled rooms,
Wondering where it went bad,
And leans to the signal, the low
Rustle of wings, the splash of an oar.

                    *

Today is one of those days
One swears is a prophesy:
The air explicit and moist,
As though filled with unanswered prayers;
The twilight, starting to slide
Its sooty fingers along the trees;
And you, Pound,

Awash in the wrong life,
Cut loose upon the lagoon (the wind
Off-shore, and gaining), the tide going out . . .
Here is your caul and caustic,
Here is your garment,
Cold-blooded father of light—
Rise and be whole again.

Venice

Homage to Arthur Rimbaud

Laying our eggs like moths
In the cold cracks of your eyes,
Brushing your hands with our dark wings

—Desperate to attempt
An entrance, to touch that light
Which buoys you like a flame,
That it might warm our own lives—,

We cluster about your death
As though it were reachable.

For almost a hundred years
We've gathered outside your legend (and been afraid
Of what such brilliance affords;

And knew the while you were risen, your flight
Pneumatic and pure, invisible as a fever;
And knew the flight was forever,
Leaving us what we deserve:

Syllables, flowers, black ice;
The exit, the split cocoon . . .

Charleville

Homage to Baron Corvo

Of all the poses, of all the roles,
This is the one I keep: you pass
On the canal, your pope's robes
Aflame in a secret light, the four
Oars of your gondola white
As moth wings in the broken dark,
The quail-eyed fisher-boys
Sliding the craft like a coffin out to sea;
The air grows hard; the boat's wake
Settles behind you like a wasted breath.

*

(For months, Corvo, you floated through my sleep
As I tried to track you down:
That winter you lived in a doorway;
The days and nights on these back canals
You spent in a musty blanket,
Your boat both bed and refuge—
And writing always
The book, the indescribable letters . . .
Was it the vengeance only
That kept you alive, the ripe corkscrew
Twisted and deep in the bottle's throat?

One afternoon—in the late spring—I went
To San Michele, to see
The sealed drawer that holds your name,
To take you flowers, as one
Is moved to do for the dead, and found
Not even a vase to put them in.
Leaving, I spread them on the lagoon,

Ungraftable shoots of blood. There is, you said,
A collusion of things in this world . . .)

                    *

And so you escape. What books there are,
Old hustler, will never exhume you,
Nor places you stayed.
Hadrian, Nicholas Crabbe, you hide
Where the dust hides now,
Your con with its last trick turned,
Stone nightmare come round again—
Fadeout: your boat, Baron, edges
Toward the horizon, a sky where toads,
Their eyes new fire,
Alone at the landings blink and blink.

                                        Venice

Homage to X

The red earth, the light diffuse
In the flat-leaved limbs of the trees;
A cold, perpetual rain
As though from a heaving breast;
O loved ones, O angels . . .

*

The thing, as always, begins
In transit, the water infusion
Oily and phosphorescent—
The vine is a blue light,
The cup is a star.

*

In the dream you will see a city,
Foreign and repetitious,
The plants unspeakably green;
That is of no concern; your job
Is the dust, the belly-relinquishing dust.

*

It's the day before yesterday,
It's the other side of the sky:
The body that bears your number
Will not be new, will not be your own
And will not remember your name.

Prague / Prague-Strashnitz

16

The New Poem

It will not resemble the sea.
It will not have dirt on its thick hands.
It will not be part of the weather.

It will not reveal its name.
It will not have dreams you can count on.
It will not be photogenic.

It will not attend our sorrow.
It will not console our children.
It will not be able to help us.

Portrait of the Poet
in Abraham von Werdt's Dream

Outside, the Venice skyline, and stars
Half-seen through an opened window;
Inside, it's the Renaissance,
The men in hose,
The furnishings elegant, but spare;
A griffin rears in the archway;
An eagle dives from the ceiling;
And over the far wall—like Dürer's—
Two cherubs support the three
Disordered initials of my signature.

Paper is stacked in neat piles, as I
First drew them; square blocks of type, their beds
Tilted and raised, their letters reversed,
Glisten among the shadows;
Two men in the foreground work
A press, inking and setting; a third
Is washing his hands, kneeling
In front of a tub; a fourth, his right arm
Extended, adjusts the unused type;
A fifth is correcting proof.

Alone in an alcove, a sixth man, unnoticed
And unfamiliar, his strange clothes
Centuries out of date, is writing, his back turned
To what I tried to record.
The lines, a spidery darkness, move
Across the page. Now
He looks this way. And now he rises
—XYZ, his mouth says, XYZ—,
Thrusting the paper into my hands.
These words are the words he has written.

Chinoiserie

Why not? The mouths of the ginger blooms slide open,
The willows drag their knuckles across the earth;
Each year has its fields that no one tends.

Our days, unlike the long gasps of the wind,
Stay half in love with the rushes, and half with the water reeds.
Outside the body, all things are encumbrances.

One Two Three

A shift in the wind the darkness
Beading about your eyelids
The sour pull of the blood
Everything works against you
The way the evening comes down
Its trellises one rose at a time
The watery knots of light
That lap at your memory
The way you thought of your life once
An endless falling of seeds

*

Already places exist
Which cannot reshelter you
Hands you have clasped for the last time
Familiar mirrors remain
That will not contain your face
Words you have uttered
That will not remember your tongue
The sofas that held your sleep
Gradually rise to assume
Their untouched shapes and their dreams

*

The wave will deliver you
Your arms thrown out like driftwood the shore
Eroding away at your touch
Your fingers ingrained in its loose skin
The idea of absence
Sprouting like grass from your side
Your autobiography
Completed no less than what
Always you claimed it would be the stone
That no one will roll away

White

Carafe, compotier, sea shell, vase:
Blank spaces, white objects;
Luminous knots along the black rope.

*

The clouds, great piles of oblivion, cruise
Over the world, the wind at their backs
Forever. They darken whomever they please.

*

The angel, his left hand on your left shoulder;
The bones, in draped white, at the door;
The bed-sheets, the pillow-case, your eyes.

*

I write your name for the last time in this mist,
White breath on the windowpane,
And watch it vanish. No, it stays there.

*

White, and the leaf clicks; dry rock;
White, and the wave spills.
Dogwood, the stripe, headlights, teeth.

Firstborn

—Omnia quae sunt, lumina sunt—

1.

The sugar dripping into your vein;
The jaundice rising upon your face like a blush;
The glass box they keep you in—

The bandage over your eyes;
The curdled milk on your lips;
The plastic tube in your throat—

The unseen hands that linger against your skin;
The name, like a new scar, at your wrist;
The glass box they keep you in—

We bring what we have to bring;
We give what we have to give;
Welcome, sweet Luke, to your life.

2.

The bougainvillaea's redress
Pulses throughout the hillside, its slow
Network of vines

Holding the earth together, giving it breath;
Outside your window, hibiscus and columbine
Tend to their various needs;

The summer enlarges.
                          You, too, enlarge,
Becoming accessible,
Your liquid reshufflings

Protracted and ill defined,
Yet absolute after all, the new skin
Blossoming pink and clear.

3.

You lie here beside me now,
Ineffable, elsewhere still.
What should one say to a son?

Emotions and points of view, the large
Abstractions we like to think
We live by—or would live by if things

Were other than what they are;
Or we were; or others were;
If all were altered and more distinct?

Or something immediate,
Descriptive, the virtuous use of words?
What can one say to a son?

4.

If it were possible, if
A way had been overlooked
To pull that rib of pure light

Out of its cage, those few felicitous vowels
Which expiate everything . . .
But nothing has been left out,

Nothing been overlooked.
The words remain in the dark, and will
Continue to glitter there;

No tricks we try to invent,
No strategies, can now extract them.
And dust is dust for a long time.

5.

What I am trying to say
Is this—I tell you, only, the thing
That I have come to believe:

Indenture yourself to the land;
Imagine you touch its raw edges
In all weather, time and again;

Imagine its colors; try
to imitate, day by day,
The morning's growth and the dusk,

The movement of all their creatures;
Surrender yourself, and be glad;
This is the law that endures.

6.

The foothills of Tennessee,
The mountains of North Carolina,
Their rivers and villages

—Hiwassee and Cherokee,
The Cumberland, Pisgah and Nantahala,
Unaka and Unicoi—

Brindle and sing in your blood;
Their sounds are the sounds you hear,
Their shapes are the shapes you see

Regardless, whenever you concentrate
Upon the remembered earth
—All things that are are lights.

Slides of Verona

1. Here where Catullus sat like snow
   Over the Adige the blooms drift
   West on the west-drifting wind

2. Cangrande mellifluous ghost sails
   His stone boat above the yard

3. St George and Trebizond each
   Elsewhere still hold their poses still burn

4. Death with its long tongue licks
   Mastino's hand affection he thinks
   Such sweetness such loyalty

5. Here comes Whatever Will Come
   His shoulders hunched under lost baggage

6. Two men their necks broken hang
   Opposite where the hill once was
   And that's where the rainbow ends

7. The star of the jasmine plant
   Who follows you now who leads

8. The great gates like wings unfold
   The angel gives him a push
   The rosaries click like locks

9. White glove immaculate touch
   How cold you are how quiet

Grace

Its hair is a fine weed,
Matted, where something has lain,
Or fallen repeatedly:

Its arms are rivers that sink
Suddenly under the earth,
Elbow and wristbone: cold sleeve:

Its face is a long soliloquy,
A language of numerals,
Impossible to erase.

Negatives

This is the light we dream in,
The milk light of midnight, the full moon
Reversing the balance like shapes on a negative:
The chalk hills, the spectral sky,
The black rose in flame,
Its odors and glittery hooks
Waiting for something to snag.

The mulberries wink like dimes;
Fat sheep, the mesquite and chaparral
Graze at their own sweet speed,
The earth white sugar;
Two miles below, and out,
The surf has nothing to add.

—Is this what awaits us, amorphous
Cobalt and zinc, a wide tide
Of brilliance we cannot define
Or use, and leafless, without guilt;
No guidelines or flutter, no
Cadence to pinpoint, no no?

Silence. As though the doorway behind
Us were liquid, were black water;
As though we might enter; as though
The ferry were there,
Ready to take us across,
—Remembering now, unwatermarked—
The blackout like scarves in our new hair.

The Fever Toy

The arms seem clumsy at first,
Outsize, the eyes detached; at odd angles,
The wrists respond to no touch;
Rickety, flat-veined, the legs
Push out like stems from their bulbous feet;
The fingers repeat themselves.

What pleasure this gives, this sure
Mating of parts, this slip and catch
Of bone to bone, of stiff flesh
To socket and joint, this gift
You give yourself in advance.
Instructions are not enclosed, and yet

How well you assemble it,
How well you insert yourself in each
Corner and crevice of its wrong arms:
Its breath caresses your eyes,
Its lips—like larvae—explore your face,
Its lashes become your own.

And this is how it begins.
This is the way your true name
Returns and returns again,
Your sorrow becoming a foreign tongue,
Your body becoming a foreign tongue,
Blue idiom, blue embrace.

Notes for Oscar Wilde at San Miniato

1.

These wings of clear flame (like dying fires,
Like vanishing wakes,
The lost light
Down there—the river?—grotesque, . . .

2.

Florence: a vortex, a mouth,
Vertiginous hive . . .

Nocturne

Florence, verticillate throat,
A hiss of enfolding wings,
The tortuous river enflamed,
The water like scales in the fire's flare . . .

3.

The fire's wings, the cries,
The long wakes of ever-diminishing light;
Below, grotesque and wide, the river
Flashes and burns like a snake;
The sudden faces of thieves, their laughter;
I stand, on San Miniato's steps,
Between two cypress, two wicks,
Two guttered and useless flames . . .

—After Dino Campana

Oscar Wilde at San Miniato

Unnatural city, monastic transparency,
Below me (in flames, the tide-lines of light
Lapping the night's brim)
You sift your impossible loves,
Your rich, suicidal dreams.
Beside the steps where I climb, four youths,
Mocking and drunk with scorn,
Flip their invisible coins.
The river flashes and winks.
Insatiable disillusion,
Dark ship, I watch the candescent fevers rise
Which burn you, rise and reflare.
Black hull, your bodies are burning like lamps,
Their bones death's rattle under the lunar fire.

—After Dino Campana

Nocturne

Florence, abyss of enfolding light:
*

The tram-lines, like wings of fire—
Their long, retreating sparks, their susurrant cries:
*

The Arno, glittering snake, touches
The white cloisters of flame, easing
Its burden, the chill of its scales:
*

The double cypress, extinguished theories
Harsher than hedgerows, harsher
Than alms-boxes; harsher, too,
Than songs my pandering heart
Continues to sing, snatches of melody:
*

—I love the old-fashioned whores
Swollen with sperm
Who plop, like enormous toads, on all fours
Over the featherbed
And wait, and puff, and snort,
Flaccid as any bellows—:
*

&c. &c. &c. &c. &c. &c. &c. &c. &c. &c.

—After Dino Campana

34

Yellow

Yellow is for regret, the distal, the second hand:
The grasshopper's wing, that yellow, the slur of dust;
Back light, the yellow of loneliness;
The yellow of animals, their yellow eyes;
The holy yellow of death;
Intuitive yellow, the yellow of air;
The double yellow, telling who comes and who goes;
The yellow of yellowhammers, one drop of the devil's blood;
The yellow of what is past;
Yellow of wormwood, yellow of straw;
The yellow of circuits, the yellow beneath the skin;
The yellow of pencils, their black veins;
Amaranth yellow, bright bloom;
The yellow of sulfur, the finger, the road home.

Dog Creek Mainline

Dog Creek: cat track and bird splay,
Spindrift and windfall; woodrot;
Odor of muscadine, the blue creep
Of kingsnake and copperhead;
Nightweed; frog spit and floating heart,
Backwash and snag pool: Dog Creek

Starts in the leaf reach and shoal run of the blood;
Starts in the falling light just back
Of the fingertips; starts
Forever in the black throat
You ask redemption of, in wants
You waken to, the odd door:

Its sky, old empty valise,
Stands open, departure in mind; its three streets,
Y-shaped and brown,
Go up the hills like a fever;
Its houses link and deploy
—This ointment, false flesh in another color.

*

Five cutouts, five silhouettes
Against the American twilight; the year
Is 1941; remembered names
—Rosendale, Perry and Smith—
Rise like dust in the deaf air;
The tops spin, the poison swells in the arm:

The trees in their jade death-suits,
the birds with their opal feet,
Shimmer and weave on the shoreline;

The moths, like forget-me-nots, blow
Up from the earth, their wet teeth
Breaking the dark, the raw grain;

The lake in its cradle hums
The old songs: out of its ooze, their heads
Like tomahawks, the turtles ascend
And settle back, leaving their chill breath
In blisters along the bank;
Locked in their wide drawer, the pike lie still as knives.

*

Hard freight. It's hard freight
From Ducktown to Copper Hill, from Six
To Piled High: Dog Creek is on this line,
Indigent spur; cross-tie by cross-tie it takes
You back, the red wind
Caught at your neck like a prize:

(The heart is a hieroglyph;
The fingers, like praying mantises, poise
Over what they have once loved;
The ear, cold cave, is an absence,
Tapping its own thin wires;
The eye turns in on itself.

The tongue is a white water.
In its slick ceremonies the light
Gathers, and is refracted, and moves
Outward, over the lips,
Over the dry skin of the world.
The tongue is a white water.).

Blackwater Mountain

That time of evening, weightless and disparate,
When the loon cries, when the small bass
Jostle the lake's reflections, when
The green of the oak begins
To open its robes to the dark, the green
Of water to offer itself to the flames,
When lily and lily pad
Husband the last light
Which flares like a white disease, then disappears:
This is what I remember. And this:

The slap of the jacklight on the cove;
The freeze-frame of ducks
Below us; your shots; the wounded flop
And skid of one bird to the thick brush;
The moon of your face in the fire's glow;
The cold; the darkness. Young,
Wanting approval, what else could I do?
And did, for two hours, waist-deep in the lake,
The thicket as black as death,
Without success or reprieve, try.

The stars over Blackwater Mountain
Still dangle and flash like hooks, and ducks
Coast on the evening water;
The foliage is like applause.
I stand where we stood before and aim
My flashlight down to the lake. A black duck
Explodes to my right, hangs, and is gone.
He shows me the way to you;
He shows me the way to a different fire
Where you, black moon, warm your hands.

Sky Valley Rider

Same place, same auto-da-fe:
Late August, the air replete, the leaves
Grotesque in their limp splendor,
The dust like guilt on the window sills,
On the pressed pants of suits
Hung like meat on their black hooks:

I walked these roads once, two steps
Behind my own life, my pockets stuffed with receipts
For goods I'd never asked for:
Complacency, blind regret; belief;
Compassion I recognized in the left palm;
Respect, slick stick, in the right:

One I have squandered, one
I have sloughed like a cracked skin; the others,
Small charms against an eventual present,
I keep in the camphor box
Beside my handkerchiefs, the slow roll
Of how I'll unravel, signatures.

*

The tinkly hymns, the wrong songs:
This one's for you, 15, lost
On the wide waters that circle beneath the earth;
You touched me once, but not now,
Your fingers like blue streamers, the stump
Of your hand, perhaps, in time to that music still:

Down by the haying shed, the white pines
Commence with their broomy sounds;
The orchard, the skeletal trunks on Anne's Ridge

—Stone and stone-colored cloud—
Gather the light and hold fast;
Two thousand acres of loneliness:

Leaf over leaf, the green sky:
Sycamore, black gum, oak, ash;
Wind-scythe at work in the far fields;
In the near, plum-flame of larkspur:
Whatever has been, remains—
Fox fire, pale semaphore in the skull's night.

*

The past, wrecked accordion, plays on, its one tune
My song, its one breath my breath,
The square root, the indivisible cipher . . .

Sex

The Holston lolls like a tongue here, its banks
Gummy and ill at ease; across the state line,
Moccasin Gap declines in a leafy sneer.
Darkness, the old voyeur, moistens his chapped lips.

Unnoticed by you, of course, your mind
Elsewhere and groping: *the stuck clasp, her knees,*
The circle around the moon, O anything . . .
—Black boat you step from, the wet's slow sift.

Then Nothing, sleek fish, nuzzles the surface calm.
The fireflies drag and relight.
The wound is unwound, the flash is tipped on the fuse,
And on the long, long waters of What's Left.

Northhanger Ridge

Half-bridge over nothingness,
White sky of the palette knife; blot orange,
Vertical blacks; blue, birdlike,
Drifting up from the next life,
The heat-waves, like consolation, wince—
One cloud, like a trunk, stays shut
Above the horizon; off to the left, dream-wires,
Hill-snout like a crocodile's.

Or so I remember it,
Their clenched teeth in their clenched mouths,
Their voices like shards of light,
Brittle, unnecessary.
Ruined shoes, roots, the cabinet of lost things:
This is the same story,
Its lips in flame, its throat a dark water,
The page stripped of its meaning.

*

Sunday, and Father Dog is turned loose:
Up the long road the children's feet
Snick in the dust like raindrops; the wind
Excuses itself and backs off; inside, heat
Lies like a hand on each head;
Slither and cough. Now Father Dog
Addles our misconceptions, points, preens,
His finger a white flag, run up, run down.

Bow-wow and arf, the Great Light;
O, and the Great Yes, and the Great No;
Redemption, the cold kiss of release,
&c.; sentences, sentences.
(Meanwhile, docile as shadows, they stare
From their four corners, looks set:
No glitter escapes
This evangelical masonry.)

*

Candleflame; vigil and waterflow:
Like dust in the night the prayers rise:
From 6 to 6, under the sick Christ,
The children talk to the nothingness,
Crossrack and wound; the dark room
Burns like a coal, goes
Ash to the touch, ash to the tongue's tip;
Blood turns in the wheel:

Something drops from the leaves; the drugged moon
Twists and turns in its sheets; sweet breath
In a dry corner, the black widow reknits her dream.
Salvation again declines,
And sleeps like a skull in the hard ground,
Nothing for ears, nothing for eyes;
It sleeps as it's always slept, without
Shadow, waiting for nothing.

Bible Camp, 1949

Primogeniture

The door to the book is closed;
The window which gives on the turned earth is closed;
The highway is closed;
Closed, too, are the waters, their lips sealed;
The door to the grass is closed.

Only the chute stays open,
The ruined chute, entering heaven—
Toehold and handhold, the wind like an accident,
The rain like mosquitoes inside your hair,
You stall still, you suffer it not.

—Rose of the afterlife, black mulch we breathe,
Devolve and restore, raise up:
Fireblight and dead bud; rust; spot;
Sore skin and shot hole:
Rechannel these tissues, hold these hands.

Nightdream

Each day is an iceberg,
Dragging its chill paunch underfoot;
Each night is a tree to hang from,
The wooden knife, the mud rope
You scratch your initials on—
Panoply, panoply.

Up and up from his green grave, your father
Wheels in the wind, split scrap of smoke;
Under him stretch, in one file, Bob's Valley, Bald Knob,
The infinite rectitude
Of all that is past: Ouachita,
Ocoee, the slow slide of the Arkansas.

Listen, the old roads are taking flight;
Like bits of string, they, too,
Rise in the pendulous sky,
Whispering, whispering:
Echo has turned a deaf ear,
The wayside is full of leaves.

Your mother floats from her bed
In slow-motion, her loose gown like a fog
Approaching, offering
Meat; across the room, a hand
Again and again
Rises and falls back, clenching, unclenching.

The chambers you've reached, the stones touched,
All stall and worm to a dot;
Sirens drain through the night; lights
Flick and release; the fields, the wet stumps,
Shed their hair and retire;
The bedroom becomes a rose:

(In Kingsport, beneath the trees,
A Captain is singing Dixie; sons
Dance in their gold suits, clapping their hands;
And mothers and fathers, each
In a soft hat, fill
With dust-dolls their long boxes).

Congenital

Here is where it begins here
In the hawk-light in the quiet
The blue of the shag spruce
Lumescent
          night-rinsed and grand

It ends in the afterdamp the rails
Shinned the saltlamps unworkable
It ends in anatomy
In limp wheels in a wisp of skin

—These hands are my father's hands these eyes
Excessively veined his eyes
Unstill ever-turning
The water the same song and the touch

Clinchfield Station

The road unwinds like a bandage.
These are the benchmarks:
A letter from Yucatan, a ball,
The chairs of the underlife.

Descent is a fact of speech,
A question of need—lampblack, cold-drill,
A glint in the residue:
Dante explained it, how

It bottoms out, becoming a threshold,
The light like a damp confetti,
The wind an apostrophe, the birds
Stone bone in the smooth-limbed trees.

*

Mums in a vase, flakes in a hope chest:
Father advise us, sift our sins—
Ferry us back and step down;
Dock at the Clinchfield Station:

Our Lady of Knoxville reclines there
On her hard bed; a golf club
Hums in the grass. The days, dry cat tracks, come round,
A silence beneath the leaves:

The way back is always into the earth.
Hornbeam or oak root, the ditch, the glass:
It all comes to the same thing:
A length of chain, a white hand.

BLOODLINES

Virgo Descending

Through the viridian (and black of the burnt match),
Through ox-blood and ochre, the ham-colored clay,
Through plate after plate, down
Where the worm and the mole will not go,
Through ore-seam and fire-seam,
My grandmother, senile and 89, crimpbacked, stands
Like a door ajar on her soft bed,
The open beams and bare studs of the hall
Pink as an infant's skin in the floating dark;
Shavings and curls swing down like snowflakes across her face.

My aunt and I walk past. As always, my father
Is planning rooms, dragging his lame leg,
Stroke-straightened and foreign, behind him,
An aberrant 2-by-4 he can't fit snug.
I lay my head on my aunt's shoulder, feeling
At home, and walk on.
Through arches and door jambs, the spidery wires
And coiled cables, the blueprint takes shape:
My mother's room to the left, the door closed;
My father's room to the left, the door closed—

Ahead, my brother's room, unfinished;
Behind, my sister's room, also unfinished.
Buttresses, winches, block-and-tackle: the scale of everything
Is enormous. We keep on walking. And pass
My aunt's room, almost complete, the curtains up,
The lamp and the medicine arranged
In their proper places, in arm's reach of where the bed will go . . .

The next one is mine, now more than half done,
Cloyed by the scent of jasmine,
White-gummed and anxious, their mouths sucking the air dry.

Home is what you lie in, or hang above, the house
Your father made, or keeps on making,
The dirt you moisten, the sap you push up and nourish . . .
I enter the living room, it, too, unfinished, its far wall
Not there, opening on to a radiance
I can't begin to imagine, a light
My father walks from, approaching me,
Dragging his right leg, rolling his plans into a perfect curl.
That light, he mutters, that damned light.
We can't keep it out. It keeps on filling your room.

Easter, 1974

Against the tin roof of the back porch, the twilight
Backdrops the climbing rose, three
Blood stars, redemptive past pain.

Trust in the fingernail, the eyelash,
The bark that channels the bone.
What opens will close, what hungers is what goes half-full.

Cancer Rising

It starts with a bump, a tiny bump, deep in the throat.
The mockingbird knows: she spreads it around
Like music, like something she's heard, a gossip to be
Repeated, but not believed.
And the bump grows, and the song grows, the song
Ascendant and self-reflective, its notes
Obscuring the quarter-tone, the slick flesh and the burning.
And the bump drops off and disappears, but
Its roots do not disappear—they dig on through the moist meat.

The roots are worms, worms in a cheese.
And what they leave, in their blind passage,
Filtered, reorganized, is a new cheese, a cheese
For one palate and one tongue.
But this takes time, and comes later,
The small mounds, heaps of a requisite sorrow,
Choked and grown in the beds,
The channels no longer channels, but flesh of a kind
Themselves, the same flesh and the song . . .

Midnight again, the mockingbird, high
In the liquidambar, runs through her scales. What burdens
Down-shift and fall, their weights sprung:
The start, the rise, the notes
Oil for the ear of death, oil for the wind, the corpse
Sailing into the universe, the geranium . . .
The music, like high water, rises inexorably . . .
Toward heaven, that intergalactic queasiness
Where all fall to the same riff.

Tallow, tallow and ash. The fire winds
Like a breath through the bone, a common tune,
Hummable, hard to extrapolate:
That song again, the song of burnt notes.
The blue it rises into, the cobalt,
Proves an enduring flame: Persian death bowl,
The bead, crystal
And drowned delta, Ephesian reed.
Blue of the twice-bitten rose, blue of the dove . . .

Tattoos

1.

Necklace of flame, little dropped hearts,
Camellias: I crunch you under my foot.
And here comes the wind again, bad breath
Of thirty-odd years, and catching up. Still,
I crunch you under my foot.

Your white stalks sequester me,
Their roots a remembered solitude.
Their mouths of snow keep forming my name.
Programmed incendiaries,
Fused flesh, so light your flowering,

So light the light that fires you
—Petals of horn, scales of blood—,
Where would you have me return?
What songs would I sing,
And the hymns . . . What garden of wax statues . . .

1973

2.

The pin oak has found new meat,
The linkworm a bone to pick.
Lolling its head, slicking its blue tongue,
The nightflower blooms on its one stem;
The crabgrass hones down its knives:

Between us again there is nothing. And since
The darkness is only light
That has not yet reached us,
You slip it on like a glove.
Duck soup, you say. *This is duck soup.*

And so it is.
                    Along the far bank
Of Blood Creek, I watch you turn
In that light, and turn, and turn,
Feeling it change on your changing hands,
Feeling it take. Feeling it.

1972

3.

Body fat as my forearm, blunt-arrowed head
And motionless, eyes
Sequin and hammer and nail
In the torchlight, he hangs there,
Color of dead leaves, color of dust,

Dumbbell and hourglass—copperhead.
Color of bread dough, color of pain, the hand
That takes it, that handles it
—The snake now limp as a cat—
Is halfway to heaven, and in time.

Then Yellow Shirt, twitching and dancing,
Gathers it home, handclap and heartstring,
His habit in ecstasy.
Current and godhead, hot coil,
Grains through the hourglass glint and spring.

1951

58

4.

Silt fingers, silt stump and bone.
And twice now, in the drugged sky,
White moons, black moons.
And twice now, in the gardens,
The great seed of affection.

Liplap of Zuan's canal, blear
Footfalls of Tintoretto; the rest
Is brilliance: Turner at 3 a.m.; moth lamps
Along the casements. O blue
Feathers, this clear cathedral . . .

And now these stanchions of joy,
Radiant underpinning:
Old scaffolding, old arrangements,
All fall in a rain of light.
I have seen what I have seen.

1968

5.

Hungering acolyte, pale body,
The sunlight—through St Paul of the 12 Sorrows—
Falls like Damascus òn me:
I feel the gold hair of Paradise rise through my skin
Needle and thread, needle and thread;

I feel the worm in the rose root.
I hear the river of heaven
Fall from the air, I hear it enter the wafer
And sink me, the whirlpool stars
Spinning me down, and down. O . . .

Now I am something else, smooth,
Unrooted, with no veins and no hair, washed
In the waters of nothingness;
Anticoronal, released . . .
And then I am risen, the cup, new sun, at my lips.

1946

6.

Skyhooked above the floor, sucked
And mummied by salt towels, my left arm
Hangs in the darkness, bloodwood, black gauze,
The slow circle of poison
Coming and going through the same hole . . .

Sprinkle of rain through the pine needles,
Shoosh pump shoosh pump of the heart;
Bad blood, bad blood . . .
                              Chalk skin like a light,
Eyes thin dimes, whose face
Comes and goes at the window?

Whose face . . .
                    For I would join it,
And climb through the nine-and-a-half footholds of fever
Into the high air,
and shed these clothes and renounce,
Burned over, repurified.

1941

61

7.

This one's not like the other, pale, gingerly—
Like nothing, in fact, to rise, as he does,
In three days, his blood clotted,
His deathsheet a feather across his chest,
His eyes twin lenses, and ready to unroll.

Arm and a leg, nail hole and knucklebone,
He stands up. In his right hand,
The flagstaff of victory;
In his left, the folds of what altered him.
And the hills spell V, and the trees V . . .

Nameless, invisible, what spins out
From this wall comes breath by breath,
And pulls the vine, and the ringing tide,
The scorched syllable from the moon's mouth.
And what pulls them pulls me.

1963

8.

A tongue hangs in the dawn wind, a wind
That trails the tongue's voice like a banner, star
And whitewash, the voice
Sailing across the 14 mountains, snap and drift,
To settle, a last sigh, here.

That tongue is his tongue, the voice his voice:
Lifting out of the sea
Where the tongue licks, the voice starts,
Monotonous, out of sync,
Yarmulke, tfillin, tallis.

His nude body waist deep in the waves,
The book a fire in his hands, his movements
Reedflow and counter flow, the chant light
From his lips, the prayer rising to heaven,
And everything brilliance, brilliance, brilliance.

1959

9.

In the fixed crosshairs of evening,
In the dust-wallow of certitude,
Where the drop drops and the scalding starts,
Where the train pulls out and the light winks,
The tracks go on, and go on:

The flesh pulls back and snaps,
The fingers are ground and scraped clean,
Reed whistles in a green fire.
The bones blow on, singing their bald song.
It stops. And it starts again.

Theologians, Interpreters:
Song, the tracks, crosshairs, the light;
The drop that is always falling.
Over again I feel the palm print,
The map that will take me there.

1952

10.

It starts here, in a chair, sunflowers
Inclined from an iron pot, a soiled dishcloth
Draped on the backrest. A throat with a red choker
Throbs in the mirror. High on the wall,
Flower-like, disembodied,

A wren-colored evil eye stares out
At the white blooms of the oleander, at the white
Gobbets of shadow and shade,
At the white lady and white parasol, at this
Dichogamous landscape, this found chord

(And in the hibiscus and moonflowers,
In the smoke trees and spider ferns,
The unicorn crosses his thin legs,
The leopard sips at her dish of blood,
And the vines strike and the vines recoil).

1973

11.

So that was it, the rush and the take-off,
The oily glide of the cells
Bringing it up—ripsurge, refraction,
The inner spin
Trailing into the cracked lights of oblivion . . .

Re-entry is something else, blank, hard:
Black stretcher straps; the peck, peck
And click of a scalpel; glass shards
Eased one by one from the flesh;
Recisions; the long bite of the veins . . .

And what do we do with this,
Rechuted, reworked into our same lives, no one
To answer to, no one to glimpse and sing,
The cracked light flashing our names?
We stand fast, friend, we stand fast.

1958

12.

Oval oval oval oval push pull push pull . . .
Words unroll from our fingers.
A splash of leaves through the windowpanes,
A smell of tar from the streets:
Apple, arrival, the railroad, shoe.

The words, like bees in a sweet ink, cluster and drone,
Indifferent, indelible,
A hum and a hum:
Back stairsteps to God, ropes to the glass eye:
Vineyard, informer, the chair, the throne.

Mojo and numberless, breaths
From the wet mountains and green mouths; rustlings,
Sure sleights of hand,
The news that arrives from nowhere:
Angel, omega, silence, silence . . .

1945

13.

What I remember is fire, orange fire,
And his huge cock in his hand,
Touching my tiny one; the smell
Of coal dust, the smell of heat,
Banked flames through the furnace door.

Of him I remember little, if anything:
Black, overalls splotched with soot,
His voice, *honey, O, honey* . . .
And then he came, his left hand
On my back, holding me close.

Nothing was said, of course—one
Terrible admonition, and that was all . . .
And if that hand, like loosed lumber, fell
From grace, and stayed there? We give,
And we take it back. We give again . . .

1940

14.

Now there is one, and still masked;
White death's face, sheeted and shoeless, eyes shut
Behind the skull holes.
She stands in a field, her shadow no shadow,
The clouds no clouds. Call her Untitled.

*

And now there are four, white shoes, white socks;
They stand in the same field, the same clouds
Vanishing down the sky. Cat masks and mop hair
Cover their faces. Advancing, they hold hands.

*

Nine. Now there are nine, their true shadows
The judgments beneath their feet.
Black masks, white nightgowns. A wind
Is what calls them, that field, those same clouds
Lisping one syllable *I, I, I.*

1970

15.

And the saw keeps cutting,
Its flashy teeth shredding the mattress, the bedclothes,
The pillow and pillow case.
Plugged in to a socket in your bones,
It coughs, and keeps on cutting.

It eats the lamp and the bedpost.
It licks the clock with its oiled tongue,
And keeps on cutting.
It leaves the bedroom, and keeps on cutting.
It leaves the house, and keeps on cutting . . .

—Dogwood, old feathery petals,
Your black notches burn in my blood;
You flutter like bandages across my childhood.
Your sound is a sound of good-bye.
Your poem is a poem of pain.

1964

16.

All gloss, gothic and garrulous, staked
To her own tree, she takes it off,
Half-dollar an article. With each
Hike of the price, the gawkers
Diminish, spitting, rubbing their necks.

Fifteen, and staked to *my* tree,
Sap-handled, hand in my pocket, head
Hot as the carnival tent, I see it out—as does
The sheriff of Cherokee County,
Who fondles the payoff, finger and shaft.

Outside, in the gathering dark, all
Is fly buzz and gnat hum and whine of the wires;
Quick scratch of the match, cicadas,
Jackhammer insects; drone, drone
Of the blood-suckers, sweet dust, last sounds . . .

1950

17.

I dream that I dream I wake
The room is throat-deep and brown with dead moths
I throw them back like a quilt
I peel them down from the wall
I kick them like leaves I shake them I kick them again

The bride on the couch and the bridegroom
Under their gauze dust-sheet
And cover up turn to each other
Top hat and tails white veil and say as I pass
It's mother again just mother the window open

On the 10th floor going up
Is Faceless and under steam his mask
Hot-wired my breath at his heels in sharp clumps
Darkness and light darkness and light
Faceless come back O come back

1955 ff.

18.

Flash click tick, flash click tick, light
Through the wavefall—electrodes, intolerable curlicues;
Splinters along the skin, eyes
Flicked by the sealash, spun, pricked;
Terrible vowels from the sun.

And everything dry, wrung, the land flaked
By the wind, bone dust and shale;
And hills without names or numbers,
Bald coves where the sky harbors.
The dead grass whistles a tune, strangely familiar.

And all in a row, seated, their mouths biting the empty air,
Their front legs straight, and their backs straight,
Their bodies pitted, eyes wide,
The rubble quick glint beneath their feet,
The lions stare, explaining it one more time.

1959

19.

The hemlocks wedge in the wind.
Their webs are forming something—questions:
Which shoe is the alter ego?
Which glove inures the fallible hand?
Why are the apple trees in draped black?

And I answer them. In words
They will understand, I answer them:
The left shoe.
The left glove.
Someone is dead; someone who loved them is dead.

Regret is what anchors me;
I wash in a water of odd names.
White flakes from next year sift down, sift down.
I lie still, and dig in,
Snow-rooted, ooze-rooted, cold blossom.

1972

20.

You stand in your shoes, two shiny graves
Dogging your footsteps;
You spread your fingers, ten stalks
Enclosing your right of way;
You yip with pain in your little mouth.

And this is where the ash falls.
And this is the time it took to get here—
And yours, too, is the stall, the wet wings
Arriving, and the beak.
And yours the thump, and the soft voice:

The octopus on the reef's edge, who slides
His fat fingers among the cracks,
Can use you. You've prayed to him,
In fact, and don't know it.
You *are* him, and think yourself yourself.

1973

Notes to Tattoos

1. Camellias; Mother's Day; St Paul's Episcopal Church,
   Kingsport, Tennessee.
2. Death of my father.
3. Snake-handling religious service; East Tennessee.
4. Venice, Italy.
5. Acolyte; fainting at the altar; Kingsport, Tennessee.
6. Blood-poisoning; hallucination; Hiwassee, North Carolina.
7. *The Resurrection*, Piero della Francesca, Borgo San Sepolcro,
   Italy.
8. Harold Schimmel's morning prayers; Positano, Italy.
9. Temporary evangelical certitude; Christ School, Arden, North
   Carolina.
10. Visions of heaven.
11. Automobile wreck; hospital; Baltimore, Maryland.
12. Handwriting class; Palmer Method; words as 'things';
    Kingsport, Tennessee.
13. The janitor; kindergarten; Corinth, Mississippi.
14. Dream.
15. The day of my mother's funeral, in Tennessee; Rome, Italy.
16. Sideshow stripper; Cherokee County Fair, Cherokee, North
    Carolina.
17. Recurrent dream.
18. The Naxian lions; Delos, Greece.
19. Death of my father.
20. The last stanza is an adaptation of lines from Eugenio
    Montale's *Serenata Indiana*.

Hardin County

—CPW, 1904–1972

There are birds that are parts of speech, bones
That are suns in the quick earth.
There are ice floes that die of cold.
There are rivers with many doors, and names
That pull their thread from their own skins.
Your grief was something like this.

Or self-pity, I might add, as you did
When you were afraid to sleep,
And not sleep, afraid to touch your bare palm,
Afraid of the wooden dog, the rose
Bleating beside your nightstand; afraid
Of the slur in the May wind.

It wasn't always like that, not in those first years
When the moon went on without its waters,
When the cores blew out of their graves in Hardin County.
How useless it is to cry out, to try
And track that light, now
Reduced to a grain of salt in the salt snow.

I want the dirt to go loose, the east wind
To pivot and fold like a string.
I want the pencil to eat its words,
The star to be sucked through its black hole.
And everything stays the same,
Locks unpicked, shavings unswept on the stone floor.

The grass reissues its green music; the leaves
Of the sassafras tree take it and pass it on;
The sunlight scatters its small change.
The dew falls, the birds smudge on their limbs.
And, over Oak Hill, the clouds, those mansions of nothingness,
Keep to their own appointments, and hurry by.

Delta Traveller

—MWW, 1910–1964

Born in the quarter-night, brash
Tongue on the tongueless ward, the moon down,
The lake rising on schedule and Dr Hurt
Already across the water, and headed home—
And so I came sailing out, first child,
A stream with no bed to lie in,
A root with no branch to leaf,
The black balloon of promise tied to your wrist,
One inch of pain and an inch of light.

*

No wonder the children stand by those moist graves.
And produce is spread on the cobbled streets,
And portraits are carried out, and horns play.
And women, in single file, untangle
Corn from the storage bins, and soft cheese.
I shield my eyes against the sunlight,
Holding, in one hand, a death's-head,
Spun sugar and marzipan. I call it Love,
And shield my eyes against the sunlight.

*

I lie down with you, I rise up with you.
If a grain turns in my eye,
I know it is you, entering, leaving,
Your name like a lozenge upon my tongue.
You drift through the antilife,
Scrim and snow-scud, fluff stem, hair
And tendril. You bloom in your own throat,
Frost flame in the frost dust,
One scratch on the slipstream, a closed mouth.

*

High-necked and high-collared, slumped and creased,
A dress sits in a chair. Your dress,
Or your mother's dress, a dress
On a wooden chair, in a cold room, a room
With no windows and no doors, full of the east wind.
The dress gets up, windbone and windskin,
To open the window. It is not there.
It goes to the door. It is not there.
The dress goes back and sits down. The dress gets up . . .

*

Three teeth and a thumbnail, white, white; four
Fingers that cradle a black chin;
Outline of eye-hole and nose-hole. This skull
And its one hand float up from the tar
And lime pit of dreams, night after slick night,
To lodge in the fork of the gum tree,
Its three teeth in the leaflight,
Its thumbnail in flash and foil,
Its mouth-hole a nothing I need to know.

*

Cat's-eye and cloud, you survive.
The porcelain corridors
That glide forever beneath your feet,
The armed lawn chair you sit in,
Your bones like paint, your skin the wrong color—
All this you survive, and hold on,
A way of remembering, a pulse
That comes and goes in the night,
Match flare and wink, that comes and goes in the night.

*

If the wafer of light offends me,
If the split tongue in the snake's mouth offends me,
I am not listening. They make the sound,
Which is the same sound, of the ant hill,
The hollow trunk, the fruit of the tree.
It is the Echo, the one transmitter of things:
Transcendent and inescapable,
It is the cloud, the mosquito's buzz,
The trickle of water across the leaf's vein.

                    *

And so with the dead, the rock dead and the dust:
Worm and worm-fill, pearl, milk-eye
And light in the earth, the dead are brought
Back to us, piece by piece—
Under the sponged log, inside the stump,
They shine with their secret lives, and grow
Big with their messages, wings
Beginning to stir, paths fixed and hearts clocked,
Rising and falling back and rising.

Skins

1.

Whatever furrow you dig in the red earth,
Whatever the tree you hang your lights on,
There comes that moment
When what you are is what you will be
Until the end, no matter
What prayer you answer to—a life
Of margins, white of the apple, white of the eye,
No matter how long you hold your hands out.
You glance back and you glance back. Ahead, in the distance, a cry
Skreeks like chalk on a blackboard.
Through riprap or backfill, sandstone or tidedrift,
You go where the landshed takes you,
One word at a time, still
Counting your money, wearing impermanent clothes.

2.

In the brushstroke that holds the angel's wing
Back from perfection; in
The synapse of word to word; in the one note
That would strike the infinite ear
And save you; and in
That last leap, the sure and redeeming edge . . .
In all beauty there lies
Something inhuman, something you can't know:
In the pith and marrow of every root
Of every bloom; in the blood-seam
Of every rock; in the black lung of every cloud
The seed, the infinitesimal seed
That dooms you, that makes you nothing,
Feeds on its self-containment and grows big.

3.

And here is the ledge,
A white ledge on a blue scarp, blue sky
Inseparable in the definition; a lens
Is tracking inexorably toward you.
Your shadow trails like a train
For miles down the glacierside, your face into view
Obliquely, then not at all,
Eyes thumbed, lips like pieces of cut glass:
This is the fair print:
Take it, eat it, it is your body and blood,
Your pose and your sacrifice; it is
Your greed and your sustenance . . .
The lens retracks, the shot unmistakable.
Take it, and be glad.

4.

First came geometry, and its dish of sparks,
Then the indifferent blue.
Then God, Original Dread, Old Voodoo Wool,
Lock-step and shadow-sprung,
Immense in the oily wind . . .
Later, the gatherings: ice, dust and its fiery hair,
The seeds in their endless scattering . . .
This linkage is nondescript
But continuing, the stars drifting into the cold
Like the corpses of Borneo
Set forth on their own rafts, washing into oblivion;
Like the reliquary tears
Of prophets, falling and falling away,
Back to geometry, back to its dish of ash.

5.

Nevertheless, the wheel arcs; nevertheless,
The mud slides and the arms yearn;
Nevertheless, you turn your face
Toward the black stone, the hard breath on the lip of God,
And find cloud, the clot you can't swallow,
The wishbone you can't spit out.
And move on, to the great fall of water;
And the light that moves there, and the click:
In the shallows, the insects,
Quick kernels of darkness, pale and explain themselves; newts
Shuttle their lanterns through the glassy leaves;
The crayfish open their doors;
The drenched wings of sunclusters rise
Like thousands of tiny cathedrals into their new language . . .

6.

Under the rock, in the sand and the gravel run;
In muck bank and weed, at the heart of the river's edge:
Instar, and again, instar,
The wing cases visible. Then
Emergence: leaf drift and detritus; skin split,
The image forced from the self.
And rests, wings drying, eyes compressed,
Legs compressed, constricted
Beneath the dun and the watershine—
Incipient spinner, set for the take-off . . .
And does, in clean tear: imago rising out of herself
For the last time, slate-winged and many-eyed.
And joins, and drops to her destiny,
Flesh to the surface, wings flush on the slate film.

7.

Sucked in and sucked out, tidewash
Hustles its razzmatazz across the cut lips
Of coral, the thousands of tiny punctures
Spewing and disappearing . . .
Where is that grain of sand that Blake saw,
The starfish that lights the way?
Pools and anemones open and close . . .
And now, on the sea's black floor,
A hand is turning your card,
One card, one turn: two dogs bark at the moon;
The crab resets her glass clock.
The weight of the sea
Is killing: you pack it forever. Shift it, sluff it;
You pack it, blue mother, forever.

8.

Something has grazed your cheek, your foot and your fingertips:
The tedious scarf of sleep, adrift
Through the afternoon. At one end, a lizard
Darts from a red rock into shade;
At the other, birds rise in the rank, inveterate blue.
July, and the olive is silhouette. The lake
Shrugs its shoulders, and goes on
Slapping its palms on the wet shale, goes on
Washing its laundry. Under
The fish-silver flash of the olive leaves, poppies
Crane up with their one good eye, and do
Nothing; the bees drag their yellow slumber.
Small pleasures: the poor man's pickpurse, the rich man's
    cutthroat.
Grainout . . . And so what? You're only passing through.

9.

The earth is what salivates, what sticks like a new glue.
It is to walk on, it is to lie down in,
A sure sheet for the resurrection.
The earth is what follows you,
Tracing your footsteps, counting your teeth, father
And son, father and grandson,
A knife, a seed, each planted just deep enough.
You start there. The birds from your sleeve burst into flame;
Your shoes catch fire, your good shoes;
Your socks sink in the dirt, all pain gone;
Your ankles sink in the dirt, your shinbones, your legs . . .
Necessity's after-breeder,
Inflamed like asparagus in the night field,
You try for the get-away by the light of yourself.

10.

Androgynous tincture, *prima materia*;
The quintessential reprieve
And coupling; sod-lifting, folly and light
In the crucible, and in the air;
And in the crosswinds, the details of diffidence . . .
This is the stung condition, and silencer:
To have come this far, to have got the jump,
The radiant archipelagos
From fog into fog beneath your body streaming—
And abstract from this
Fabric, this silkscreen that patterns you
(The chancelled dawn, vast
Surplice and undershine), one glint of the golden stitch,
The thread that will lead you home:

11.

Upriver, then, past landfall and watertrace,
Past wheels, past time and its bufferings . . .
A clearing appears; reed huts
Extend from the jungle face, its vinelap and overbite;
Out of them step, in cadence—a slip skip slip—,
Two men with their six-foot flutes, two women behind them,
Their dance, their song ascending like smoke and light
Back to the sky, back to the place it came from . . .
Of course, it's unworkable.
Better to dig a round hole in the earth, be lowered
And fixed in the clay in a stranger's arms;
Be covered with thick feathers,
Your stiff arms stiff at your sides, knees flexed,
Marked for the tilt and the blind slide.

12.

Exurgent mortui et ad me veniunt . . . .
Midnight, the Christmas Mass; and the host raised, and the
    summoned
Summoned. And then to the boneyard, eyes eastward,
Two bones in the right hand, St Andrew's cross
Pathetic against the dawn's skull.
Then north, four thousand and nineteen hundred paces,
To lie down, outstretched, hands on the legs,
Eyes heavenward, unlocked to the quarter moon:
Ego sum, te peto et videre queo . . .
And will they step from their dust?
Will they sit in their rocking chairs, decayed hands
Explaining the maps you must follow?
Will circles be explicated, the signs shriven?
The land of the chosen has one door, there is no knob . . .

13.

Naked, spindled, the hand on the chimney mantel,
Length-fingered, bud-sprouted bone:
The Hand of Glory, spread toward its one address:
The right hand, or the left hand,
Lopped at the new moon, and fresh from the gibbet;
Wrapped in a funeral pall, squeezed, palmed;
Then brought, in the dog-days, from its pot,
Pumiced by zimat, nitre and long peppers;
Then to the oven; vervain
And fern imbue its grainlessness; the candle
—Man-fat, wax, ponie and sesame—
Forks from its wonder; lighted,
It freezes the looker's reach, and locks both
The mark and beholder, ghost forms on the negative . . .

14.

They talk of a city, whose moon-colored battlements
Kneel to the traveller, whose
Windows, like after-burners, stream
Out their chemistry, applying their anodyne.
They talk of a river, its waters
A balm, an unguent unscrubbable. They talk. And they talk
Of the light that lights the stars
Through the five organs, like a wind spread by the rain.
They talk of a medicine, a speck
—Omnipotent, omnipresent, clogged
With the heavy earth and the mind's intractable screen—
To be shaken loose, dissolved, and blown
Through the veins, becoming celestial.
They talk, and nothing appears. They talk and it does not appear.

15.

And so downriver, yourself, and yourself's shadow,
All that you bring back.
Still, it's enough: sounding board, handhold,
Ear-rig and in-seeing eye . . .
Back from the seven-caved mountain, its cross
Where the serpent is nailed; back
From the oak-stock and rose, their rivulet
Sought by the blind with their dry touch; back
From the Innocents, that vat where the sun and the moon
Dip to their red bath . . .
The Echo is arbitrary: flame, wind, rainwrack
And soil, each a survivor, each one
An heir to the fingerprint, the slip of a tongue.
Each is where you begin; each one an end in itself . . .

16.

Procedure and process, the one
Inalterable circulation. First, cleared ground, swept
And unhindered; next, bark moss, pine pitch,
Their angles of termination
Exact, the boughs that are added exact; then loblolly, split
From the fall felling; then ball bats, blue shoes,
All the paraphernalia of past lives:
The headrests, the backrests, all the poor furniture . . .
As the fire builds, you enter and lie down:
You feed the flames; you feed them with all you've got:
Finger and forearm, torso,
Shoulders and hair . . . And the sparks
That rise, the cinders,
Rework you and make you new, burned to an ash.

17.

The wind hauls out its valued baggage in three steps
Tonight, and drops it with some relief
In the full dark, in the leaves of an avocado tree.
The grass rises to meet it.
As always, you, too, rise, and meet them halfway,
And nod your head, and accept
Their leavings, and give thanks, crumbs
For the tablecloth, crumbs for the plate, and wolf them down . . .
The rivers of air you've filtered and rearranged
Since birth, and paid no heed to,
Surprise you now, and start to take on
The acid and eye of what's clear,
That milky message of breath on cold mornings—
That what you take in is seldom what you let out.

18.

There is a shine you move towards, the shine
Of water; you want it to step from,
And out of, wearing its strings and slick confetti.
You come to the sea, but turn back, its surgy retractions
Too slippery, and out of place,
Wrecked looking-glass, bundles of grief.
And inland, the necklace of lakes—High Lonesome
And pendant, the 40s its throat,
Its glint like icicles against the skin . . . ?
There's no one to wear it now, or hand it down.
The river will have it, shine
Of the underlight, shine of the lost quarter;
The river, rope of remembering, unbroken shoe,
The flushed and unwaivering mirror . . .

19.

You thought you climbed, and all the while you descended.
Go up and go down; what other work is there
For you to do, what other work in this world?
The seasons back off. The hills
Debase themselves, and keep on growing. Over the land,
Your feet touch down like feathers,
A brushstroke here, a gouge there, lacking a print
Always, and always without direction.
Or so it seems. But what, for one meandering man,
Is all that, who looks for the willow's change,
The drift and slip of smoke through the poplar leaves,
The cliff's dance and wind's shift,
Alone with the owl and the night crawler
Where all is a true turning, and all is growth.

20.

You've talked to the sun and moon,
Those idols of stitched skin, bunch grass and twigs
Stuck on their poles in the fall rain;
You've prayed to Sweet Medicine;
You've looked at the Hanging Road, its stars
The stepstones and river bed where you hope to cross;
You've followed the cricket's horn
To sidestep the Lake of Pain . . .
And what does it come to, Pilgrim,
This walking to and fro on the earth, knowing
That nothing changes, or everything;
And only, to tell it, these sad marks,
Phrases half-parsed, ellipses and scratches across the dirt?
It comes to a point. It comes and it goes.

1—Situation, Point A
2—Beauty
3—Truth
4—Destruction of the universe
5—Organized religion
6—Metamorphosis
7—Water
8—Water/Earth
9—Earth/Fire
10—Aether
11—Primitive Magic
12—Necromancy
13—Black Magic
14—Alchemy
15—Allegory
16—Fire
17—Air
18—Water
19—Earth
20—Situation, Point A

Link Chain

Palm Sunday. Banana leaves
Loll in the breaklight. Back home, on Ravine Street
25 years ago, Philbeck and I
Would count the crosses, arrange
The pins on their silver plate, and bank
On a full house. The palm crosses, tiny
And off-green against their purple cloth,
Are stacked like ricks for the match flame. 11 o'clock.
I take a cross and two pins—
One for the cross, and one again for the heart.

*

On the front seat of a Yellow Coach,
Pistol Red at the wheel, 10 miles this side of Surgoinsville
On US 11-W, I'd lay my body down, in Tennessee,
For the 1st time. The 2nd time
I'd pick a tree, black cherry,
That grows on the north side of Chestnut Ridge, and looks out
Over the Cumberlands;
I'd build a floor and face west.
For number 3, I'd float in a boat downriver,
Whatever river, and be a leaf.

*

Circle by circle, link chain
And hair breath, I'm bound to the oak mulch, those leaves
Stuffed in their croker sacks
My brother and I were sent for each week-end
In autumn, in Moody's Woods, to drag back

Up Hog Hill and feed the shredder with.
Later, confettied and packed tight in their little mounds,
They warmed the milk root and the slip stalk.
Later still, and less coarse, they'll warm me,
Bone stock and finger peg, the cold room.

*

From this pocket to that pocket, bright coin
Whose slot in the crossed box was cut
38 years ago, and cut well,
I roll through the world, Peter's pence
For the red clay, defrocked and worn smooth,
The payment in someone's hand.
Lord of the Anchorite, wind-blown bird,
Dangle your strings and hook me.
I am the gleam in your good eye, I am your ticket;
Take me up, and drop me where I belong.

                    *

Each tree I look at contains my coffin,
Each train brings it closer home.
Each flower I cut, I cut for a plastic vase
Askew on the red dirt, the oak trees
Whisking their wash in the May wind.
Each root I uncover uncovers me.
Below, 19 By-pass swings straight to the state line
5 miles north, Virginia across the bridge—
Each car is the car that brings
That tree to earth, the earth to the earth again.

                    *

Big Sister, hair heaped like a fresh grave,
Turns in my arms as my arms turn,
Her fingers cool tubers against my skin

As we slide slide to the music, humming
An old tune, knee touching knee,
Step-two-three, step-two-three
Under a hard hatful of leaves,
The grass with its one good limb holding
The beat, a hint of impending form.
It gathers, it reaches back, it is caught up.

Bays Mountain Covenant

For my own speech and that which I leave unspoken
For my own death and the deaths that will follow me
For the three thrones for the sticks for the wires
For the whole hog and the half-truth
For my knot of life and its one string
That goes from this man's rumor to that one's promise
For the songs I hear and the hush I should imitate
For the sky my eye sees and the one that it cannot find
For the raising up and the setting down
For the light for the light for the light

He praised for 10 years and was suckered by
A foot in the wrong shoe a hat in the wind
Sir you will pardon him you will wave if he now turns
To the leaf to the fire in the swamp log to the rain
The acorn of crystal at the creek's edge which prove
Nothing expect nothing and offer nothing
Desire no entrance and harbor no hope of change
Foxglove that seeks no answer nightshade that seeks no answer
Not to arrive at and be part of but to take
As the water accepts the whirlpool the earth the storm

Rural Route

The stars come out to graze, wild-eyed in the new dark.
The dead squeeze close together,
Strung out like a seam of coal through the raw earth.
I smell its fragrance, I touch its velvet walls.

The willow lets down her hooks.
On the holly leaves, the smears of light
Retrench and repeat their alphabet,
That slow code. The boxwood leans out to take it on,

Quicker, but still unbroken.
Inside the house, in one room, a twelve-year-old
Looks at his face on the windowpane, a face
Once mine, the same twitch to the eye.

The willow flashes her hooks.
I step closer. Azalea branches and box snags
Drag at my pants leg, twenty-six years gone by.
I enter the wedge of light.

And the face stays on the window, the eyes unchanged.
It still looks in, still unaware of the willow, the boxwood
Or any light on any leaf. Or me.
Somewhere a tire squeals, somewhere a door is shut twice.

And what it sees is what it has always seen:
Stuffed birds on a desk top, a deer head
On the wall, and all the small things we used once
To push the twelve rings of the night back.

How silly! And still they call us
Across the decades, fog horns,
Not destinations, outposts of things to avoid, reefs
To steer clear of, pockets of great abandon.

I back off, and the face stays.
I leave the back yard, and the front yard, and the face stays.
I am back on the West Coast, in my studio,
My wife and my son asleep, and the face stays.

CHINA TRACE

Childhood

Shrunken and drained dry, turning transparent,
You've followed me like a dog
I see through at last, a window into Away-From-Here, a place
I'm headed for, my tongue loosened, tracks
Apparent, your beggar's-lice
Bleaching to crystal along my britches leg:

I'm going away now, goodbye.
Goodbye to the locust husk and the chairs;
Goodbye to the genuflections. Goodbye to the clothes
That circle beneath the earth, the names
Falling into the darkness, face
After face, like beads from a broken rosary . . .

Snow

If we, as we are, are dust, and dust, as it will, rises,
Then we will rise, and recongregate
In the wind, in the cloud, and be their issue,

Things in a fall in a world of fall, and slip
Through the spiked branches and snapped joints of the evergreens,
White ants, white ants and the little ribs.

Self-Portrait in 2035

The root becomes him, the road ruts
That are sift and grain in the powderlight
Recast him, sink bone in him,
Blanket and creep up, fine, fine:

Worm-waste and pillow tick; hair
Prickly and dust-dangled, his arms and black shoes
Unlinked and laceless, his face false
In the wood-rot, and past pause . . .

Darkness, erase these lines, forget these words.
Spider recite his one sin.

Morandi

I'm talking about stillness, the hush
Of a porcelain center bowl, a tear vase, a jug.

I'm talking about space, which is one-sided,
Unanswered, and left to dry.

I'm talking about paint, about shape, about the void
These objects sentry for, and rise from.

I'm talking about sin, red drop, white drop,
Its warp and curve, which is blue.

I'm talking about bottles, and ruin,
And what we flash at the darkness, and what for . . .

Dog

The fantailed dog of the end, the lights out,
Lopes in his sleep,
The moon's moan in the glassy fields.
Everything comes to him, stone
Pad prints extending like stars, tongue black
As a flag, saliva and thread, the needle's tooth,
Everything comes to him.

If I were a wind, which I am, if I
Were smoke, which I am, if I
Were the colorless leaves, the invisible grief,
Which I am, which I am,
He'd whistle me down, and down, but not yet.

Snapshot

Under the great lens of heaven, caught
In the flash and gun of the full moon,
Improbable target in the lunar click,

My own ghost, a lock-shot lanyard of blue flame,
Slips from the deadeyes in nothing's rig,
Raiment and sustenance, and hangs

Like a noose in the night wind. Or like a mouth,
O-fire in the scaffolding. You are wine
In a glass, it says, you are sack, you are silt.

Indian Summer

The plains drift on through the deep daylight.

I watch the snow bees sent mad by the sun.

The limbs of the hickory trees swing loose in the noontide,
Feathery, stretching their necks.

The wind blows through its own hair forever.

If something is due me still
—Firedogs, ashes, the soap of another life—
I give it back. And this hive

Of sheveled combs, my wax in its little box.

Wishes

I wish I were unencumbered, in Venice or South Bay.
I wish I were thrust down by enormous weights
Anywhere, anywhere.
I wish that the blood fly would crawl from its hiding place.

The sun slides up through the heat, and has no dreams.
The days drop, each nosed by the same dog.
In some other language
I walk by this same river, these same vowels in my throat.

I wish I could say them now, returned
Through the dry thread of the leaf, the acorn's root.
It's somewhere I can't remember, but saw once.
It's late in the afternoon there, the lights coming on.

Quotidiana

The moss retracts its skin from the laced grass.
This mist is a cold address,
This late light a street that others have moved from too.
The river stays shut, and writes my biography.

Midwinter, midwinter,
Your necktie of ice, your salt shoes,
Trees in a numb nudge, you
Come through the sand sieve, you bear me up.

At Zero

In the cold kitchen of heaven,
Daylight spoons out its cream-of-wheat.

Beside the sidewalk, the shrubs
Hunch down, deep in their bibs.

The wind harps its same song
Through the steel tines of the trees.

The river lies still, the jeweled drill in its teeth.

I am glint on its fingernails.
I am ground grains on its wheel.

Sentences

The ash fish has been away for a long time now,
The snow transparent; a white cane rakes back and forth
In the hush, no sweet sound from the leaves.

———

Whatever is dead stays dead: the lighted and cold
Blue blank pavilions of the sky,
The sand, the crystal's ring in the bushy ear—
Voices logy with sleep, their knapsacks
The color of nothing, full of the great spaces they still must cross.

———

The trees take care of their own salvation, and rocks
Swell with their business: and there, on the clean cloth
Of the river, a Host is floating without end.

———

Heaven, that stray dog, eats on the run and keeps moving.

Death

I take you as I take the moon rising,
Darkness, black moth the light burns up in.

Next

I am weary of daily things,
How the limbs of the sycamore
Dip to the snow surge and disaffect;
How the ice moans and the salt swells.
Where is that country I signed for, the one with the lamp,
The one with the penny in each shoe?

I want to lie down, I am so tired, and let
The crab grass seep through my heart,
Side by side with the inchworm and the fallen psalm,
Close to the river bank,
In autumn, the red leaves in the sky
Like lost flags, sidle and drift . . .

January

In some other life
I'll stand where I'm standing now, and will look down, and will
    see
My own face, and not know what I'm looking at.

These are the nights
When the oyster begins her pearl, when the spider slips
Through his wired rooms, and the barns cough, and the grass
    quails.

1975

Year of the Half-Hinged Mouth and the Hollow Bones,
Year of the Thorn,
Year of the Rope and the Dead Coal,
Year of the Hammering Mountain, Year of the Sponge . . .

I open the book of What I Can Never Know
To page 1, and start to read:
"The snow falls from the hills to the sea, from the cloud
To the cloud's body, water to water . . ."

At 40, the apricot
Seems raised to a higher power, the fire ant and the weed.
And I turn in the wind,
Not knowing what sign to make, or where I should kneel.

Nerval's Mirror

I'll never know what the clouds promised,
Or what the stars intended to say;
I'll never return the call of What's-To-Come.

I'm safe now, and well fed.
Don't look for me in the white night of the Arctic;
I'm floating here, my side iced to its side.

Edvard Munch

We live in houses of ample weight,
Their windows a skin-colored light, pale and unfixable.
Our yards are large and windraked, their trees bent to the storm.
People we don't know are all around us.

Or else there is no one, and all day
We stand on a bridge, or a cliff's edge, looking down.
Our mothers stare at our shoes.

Hands to our ears, our mouths open, we're pulled on
By the flash black, flash black flash of the lighthouse
We can't see on the rock coast,
Notes in a bottle, our lines the ink from the full moon.

Bygones

The rain has stopped falling asleep on its crystal stems

Equation

I open the phone book, and look for my adolescence.
How easy the past is—
Alphabetized, its picture taken,
It leans in the doorway, it fits in the back pocket.

The crime is invisible,
But it's there. Why else would I feel so guilty?
Why else would that one sorrow still walk through my sleep,
Looking away, dressed in its best suit?

I touch my palm. I touch it again and again.
I leave no fingerprint. I find no white scar.
It must have been something else,
Something enormous, something too big to see.

California Twilight

Late evening, July, and no one at home.
In the green lungs of the willow, fly-worms and lightning bugs
Blood-spot the whips and wings. Blue

Asters become electric against the hedge.
What was it I had in mind?
The last whirr of a skateboard dwindles down Oak Street hill.

Slowly a leaf unlocks itself from a branch.
Slowly the furred hands of the dead flutter up from their caves.
A little pinkish flame is snuffed in my mouth.

Anniversary

At dawn, in the great meadow, a solitude
As easy as white paint comes down from the mountains
To daydream, bending the grass.

I take my body, familiar bundle of sorrows, to be
Touched by its hem, and smoothed over . . .

There's only one secret in this life that's worth knowing,
And you found it.
                        I'll find it too.

12 Lines at Midnight

Sleep, in its burning garden, sets out the small plants.
Behind me an animal breaks down,
One ear to the moon's brass sigh.

The earth ticks open like a ripe fruit.
The mist, with its sleeves of bone, slides out of the reeds,
Everything hushed, the emptiness everywhere.

The breath inside my breath is the breath of the dream.
I lick its charred heart, a piece of the same flaked sky
The badger drags to his hole.

The bread bleeds in the cupboard,
The mildew tightens. The clocks, with their tiny hands, reach out,
Inarticulate monitors of the wind.

Dino Campana

After the sad tunes on the dog's tooth,
The twistwort and starbane
—Blood lilies the heart breeds—,
Your mouth is the blue door I walk through,
The lamp lit, the table laid.

Invisible Landscape

This is the way it must have been in the first dusk:
Smokeclouds sculling into their slips in the Claw Mountains,
Bats jerked through the plumlight by strings of white sound;
The wind clicks through its turnstiles
Over the high country, the hush of a steady pulse . . .

I bring to this landscape a bare hand, these knuckles
Slick as a cake of soap,
The black snag of a tamarack,
The oddments and brown jewelry of early September evenings
In wet weather, a Colt-colored sky . . .

God is the sleight-of-hand in the fireweed, the lost
Moment that stopped to grieve and moved on . . .

Remembering San Zeno

After the end, they'll bring you
To someplace like this, columns of light propped through a west-
   facing door,
People standing about, echo of shoe-taps,
The gloom, like a grease-soaked rag, like a slipped skin
Left in a corner, puddled
In back of the votive stick stands, matter-of-factly—

Under the lisp and cold glow of the flames
Everything stares and moves closer, faces and blank hands,
October the 1st, 1975.
The banked candles the color of fresh bone,
Smoke rising from chimneys beyond the beyond,
Nightfires, your next address . . .

Born Again

Sunday night and a full moon,
October the 19th, moon glyphs on the grass and leaves.
In the endless expanse of heaven,
3 stars break out through the cover-up, and hang free.
Behind the veneer of light and the scorched lungs
Are walks I will take.

Nothingness, tilt your cup.
I am the wafer just placed on your tongue,
The transubstantiation of bone and regret
To air and a photograph;
I am the diamond and bad heart,
Breath's waste, the slip-back and failure of What's Past.

Captain Dog

Another December, another year
Gone to the bleached Pacific, a little castle of snow
Falling across the sky
I wanted to linger in for awhile.

And so I lose touch, the walls, in their iced dismemberings,
Shrinking like aches, a slide and a by-your-leave.

The nights, with their starred palms, press down,
Black moths on the screen door,
Slow breaths to stop the body's bleeding, deep breaths.

I'm jump-cut and Captain Dog, staked
In the shadow of nothing's hand.
I bend like a finger joint, I gather, I burn.

1975

Depression Before the Solstice

4 days till the solstice, the moon
Like an onion thin in the afternoon sky, the few leaves
In the liquidambar arthritic and holding on.
The weightless, unclarified light from the setting sun
Lies like despair on the ginger root. Windows
Go up in flame. Now

The watchers and holy ones set out, divining
The seal, eclipses
Taped to their sleeves with black felt,
Their footprints filling with sparks
In the bitter loam behind them, ahead of them stobbed with sand,
And walk hard, and regret nothing.

Stone Canyon Nocturne

Ancient of Days, old friend, no one believes you'll come back.
No one believes in his own life anymore.

The moon, like a dead heart, cold and unstartable, hangs by a
    thread
At the earth's edge,
Unfaithful at last, splotching the ferns and the pink shrubs.

In the other world, children undo the knots in their tally strings.
They sing songs, and their fingers blear.

And here, where the swan hums in his socket, where bloodroot
And belladonna insist on our comforting,
Where the fox in the canyon wall empties our hands, ecstatic for
    more,

Like a bead of clear oil the Healer revolves through the night
    wind,
Part eye, part tear, unwilling to recognize us.

Reply to Chi K'ang

There is no light for us at the end of the light.
No one redeems the grass our shadows lie on.

Each night, in its handful of sleep, the mimosa blooms.
Each night the future forgives.
Inside us, albino roots are starting to take hold.

Reunion

Already one day has detached itself from all the rest up ahead.
It has my photograph in its soft pocket.
It wants to carry my breath into the past in its bag of wind.

I write poems to untie myself, to do penance and disappear
Through the upper right-hand corner of things, to say grace.

"Where Moth and Rust Doth Corrupt"

No moon in the eastern sky, the Big Dipper
Spilling its nothingness from Baja to Prudhomme Bay,
Ashes strewn through my life like old clothes.
The outline of 10 crosses still dampens and stains my childhood,
Oppressive forehead, infinite hymn . . .

Lie back and regenerate,
                          family of dust,
Invisible groom, father and son I step through.
Spread for the fly's fall,
Its body released and sucked clean and full of the air.
I whisper into a different ear.

I mimic the tongues of green flame in the grass.
I live in the one world, the moth and rust in my arms.

April

The plum tree breaks out in bees.
A gull is locked like a ghost in the blue attic of heaven.
The wind goes nattering on,
Gossipy, ill at ease, in the damp rooms it will air.
I count off the grace and stays
My life has come to, and know I want less—

Divested of everything,
A downfall of light in the pine woods, motes in the rush,
Gold leaf through the undergrowth, and come back
As another name, water
Pooled in the black leaves and holding me there, to be
Released as a glint, as a flash, as a spark . . .

Signature

Don't wait for the snowfall from the dogwood tree.
Live like a huge rock covered with moss,
Rooted half under the earth
                              and anxious for no one.

Noon

I look up at the black bulge of the sky and its belt of stars,
And know I can answer to nothing in all that shine,
Desire being ash, and not remembered or brought back by the
    breath,
Scattered beneath the willow's fall, a figure of speech . . .

And know that what I have asked for cannot be granted, that what
Is waiting for me is laced in my 2 shoes,
Wind that will alter me, extension that one day will ease me on
In my slow rise through the dark toward the sweet wrists of the
    rose.

The dirt is a comforting, and the night drafts from the sucker
    vines.
The grass is a warm thing, and the hollyhocks, and the bright
    bursts from the weeds.
But best of all is the noon, and its tiny horns,
When shadows imprint, and start
                              their gradual exhalation of the past.

Going Home

The ides of a hangdog month.
Dirt roads and small towns come forth
And fall from the pepper tree,
                     evening flashing their panes
And stray flakes through a thin drizzle of darkness,
Strikes in the dry fields of the past,
                     bonesparks
From the nailed feet that walk there.

I ask for a second breath,
Great Wind, where everything's necessary
And everything rises,
                     unburdened and borne away, where
The flash from the setting sun
Is more than a trick of light, where halflife
Is more than just a watery glow,
                     and everything's fire . . .

Cloud River

The unborn children are rowing out to the far edge of the sky,
Looking for warm beds to appear in. How lucky they are, dressed
In their lake-colored gowns, the oars in their oily locks
Taking them stroke by stroke to circumference and artery . . .

I'd like to be with them still, pulling my weight,
Blisters like small white hearts in the waxed palms of my hands.
I'd like to remember my old name, and keep the watch,
Waiting for something immense and unspeakable to uncover its
    face.

Reply to Lapo Gianni

Lapo, we're all slow orphans under the cruel sleep of heaven.
We're all either creased and sealed or somebody's cough.

Outside the window, twilight slips on its suede glove.
The river is fine balsam, fragrant and nicked by cold feathers.
Under the grass, the lights go on in their marled rooms.

Lapo, the dreams of the dog rose are nothing to you and me.

Thinking of Georg Trakl

August, the bones of summer, the chamber and last lunch
Before the fall. All day the creatures and small wings
Have hung back or held their tongues.
All day they have known what we will know when the time comes.

Sister of Mercies, a body is laid out, look,
Under the ghost light of the stars. 11:15. With different breaths,
Silently, up from the river, its wet-sheet of mist
Is drawn forth and arranged.

Lips part in the bleached willows.
Finger by finger, above Orion, God's blue hand unfolds.

Spider Crystal Ascension

The spider, juiced crystal and Milky Way, drifts on his web
    through the night sky
And looks down, waiting for us to ascend . . .

At dawn he is still there, invisible, short of breath, mending his
    net.

All morning we look for the white face to rise from the lake like a
    tiny star.
And when it does, we lie back in our watery hair and rock.

Moving On

Once it was lamb's fleece and the fall.
Once it was wedge of the eyelid and eyelid down to poison and
   sheer slumber,
The flesh made flesh and the word.

Now it's the crack in the porcelain stick,
And midnight splashed on the 1st rocks and gone,
The wafer of blood in its chalk robes,

The bright nail of the east I usher my body toward.

Clear Night

Clear night, thumb-top of a moon, a back-lit sky.
Moon-fingers lay down their same routine
On the side deck and the threshold, the white keys and the black
  keys.
Bird hush and bird song. A cassia flower falls.

I want to be bruised by God.
I want to be strung up in a strong light and singled out.
I want to be stretched, like music wrung from a dropped seed.
I want to be entered and picked clean.

And the wind says "What?" to me.
And the castor beans, with their little earrings of death, say
  "What?" to me.
And the stars start out on their cold slide through the dark.
And the gears notch and the engines wheel.

Autumn

November the 1st. Gold leaves
Whisper their sentences through the blue chains of the wind.
I open a saint-john's-bread.

Green apples, a stained quilt,
The black clock of the heavens reset in the future tense.
Salvation's a simple thing.

Sitting at Night on the Front Porch

I'm here, on the dark porch, restyled in my mother's chair.
10:45 and no moon.
Below the house, car lights
Swing down, on the canyon floor, to the sea.

In this they resemble us,
Dropping like match flames through the great void
Under our feet.
In this they resemble her, burning and disappearing.

Everyone's gone
And I'm here, sizing the dark, saving my mother's seat.

Saturday 6 a.m.

The month gone and the day coming up like a bad cold
Insistent behind the eyes, a fine sweat on the mustard stalks.
There's something I want to say,

But not here, stepped out and at large on the blurred hillside.
Over my shoulder, the great pane of the sunlight tilts toward the
  sea.
I don't move. I let the wind speak.

Him

His sorrow hangs like a heart in the star-flowered boundary tree.
It mirrors the endless wind.

He feeds on the lunar differences and flies up at the dawn.

When he lies down, the waters will lie down with him,
And all that walks and all that stands still, and sleep through the
    thunder.

It's for him that the willow bleeds.

Look for him high in the flat black of the northern Pacific sky,
Released in his suit of lights,
                    lifted and laid clear.

Mingliaotse: "I would like to house my spirit within my body, to nourish my virtue by mildness, and to travel in ether by becoming a void. But I cannot do it yet . . . And so, being unable to find peace within myself, I made use of the external surroundings to calm my spirit, and being unable to find delight within my heart, I borrowed a landscape to please it. Therefore, strange were my travels."

T'u Lung (T'u Ch'ihshui)
Translated by Lin Yutang

UNIVERSITY PRESS OF NEW ENGLAND publishes books under its own imprint and is the publisher for Brandeis University Press, Dartmouth College, Middlebury College Press, University of New Hampshire, Tufts University, and Wesleyan University Press.

ABOUT THE AUTHOR

Charles Wright was born in Pickwick Dam, Tennessee, in 1935 and grew up in rural Tennessee and North Carolina. He was educated at Davidson College and the University of Iowa and began writing his first poems while serving in the Army Intelligence Service from 1957 to 1961, stationed in Verona, Italy. He then studied in Rome as a Fulbright Scholar, translating the poems of Eugenio Montale and Cesare Pavese, and taught in Padua as a Fulbright Lecturer. In 1974 he received a National Endowment for the Arts Award, and in 1975 won a Guggenheim Fellowship. For seventeen years he was a member of the English department at the University of California, Irvine. In 1983 he became Professor of English at the University of Virginia and now lives in Charlottesville with his wife, the photographer Holly Wright.

In addition to the 1983 National Book Award for *Country Music*, he has won the PEN Translation prize in 1979 for Eugenio Montale's *The Storm and Other Things*, the Academy-Institute Award in 1977, the Academy of American Poets' Edgar Allan Poe award in 1976 for *Bloodlines*, and the Brandeis Creative Arts Citation for Poetry in 1987. Besides the four early books of poetry selected from here, he published another four volumes in the 1980s—*The Southern Cross, The Other Side of the River, Zone Journals*, and *Xionia*—which have been collected in the book *The World of the Ten Thousand Things: Poems 1980-1990*.

Library of Congress Cataloging-in-Publication Data

Wright, Charles, 1935–
    Country music : early selected poems / Charles Wright. — 2nd ed.
    p.   cm.
ISBN 0-8195-1201-X (pbk.)
I. Title.
PS3573.R52C66   1991
811'.54—dc20   ∞   91–50378